Cambridge Wizard Student Guide

Gattaca

Directed by Andrew Niccol

Richard McRoberts
B.A., M.Ed., M.A.C.E.
Marcia Pope
M.A., B.Ed., Grad. Dip. Children's Lit.

CAMBRIDGE
UNIVERSITY PRESS

PUBLISHED BY THE PRESS SYNDICATE OF THE UNIVERSITY OF CAMBRIDGE
The Pitt Building, Trumpington Street, Cambridge, United Kingdom

CAMBRIDGE UNIVERSITY PRESS
The Edinburgh Building, Cambridge CB2 2RU, UK
40 West 20th Street, New York, NY 10011–4211, USA
477 Williamstown Road, Port Melbourne 3207, Australia
Ruiz de Alarcón 13, 28014 Madrid, Spain
Dock House, The Waterfront, Cape Town 8001, South Africa

http://www.cambridge.edu.au

First published in 2003
Reprinted in 2003, 2004, 2006

Cover design by Cressaid Media
Cover art by Valerie Den Ouden
Typeset by Aja Bongiorno

Printed in Australia by Print Impressions

Typeface Berkeley *System* PageMaker® [AB]

National Library of Australia Cataloguing in Publication data
      Pope, Marcia.
      Gattaca.
      For VCE English students.
      ISBN 0 521 53615 4.
      1. Gattaca (Motion picture). I. Title. (Series: Cambridge wizard students guide).
791.4372

ISBN 0 521 53615 4 paperback
Marcia Pope is an Academic Associate of the University of Ballarat (former Senior Lecturer in
Film and Media).

Contents

Notes on the Director and Crew

Andrew Niccol was born in New Zealand in 1964. After schooling, he went into television. He subsequently moved to Britain, and worked for many years making TV commercials. This taught him his craft, but proved artistically unfulfilling.

He moved to Hollywood in the mid 1990s with a new ambition to make movies that 'lasted longer than 60 seconds'. He started by writing a screenplay, *The Truman Show*. But while that project was accepted for production, delays meant that it could not begin shooting.

In the meantime, Niccol developed another script, called *Gattaca*. He 'pitched' the idea to various production houses, and was taken up by the independent Jersey Films. The company, a partnership of actor/director Danny de Vito and producers Michael Shamberg and Stacey Sher, had already enjoyed considered critical and commercial success, with hits like *Reality Bites*, *Pulp Fiction*, *Get Shorty* and *Fierce Creatures*. They were attracted by the way the script combined strong genre elements with a stimulating idea. Says Shamberg:

Quote

The story was mesmerising. It's a world that is all-encompassing, so you enter it not just for the good character story that it has but also for this picture of the future that you're anxious to see. I call it 'social science fiction' – alternative futures written in a believable way. But Niccol also combines this alternate reality with such great movie elements as a mystery, a love story and a thriller. (Production Notes).

The script was accepted, and Niccol taken on as director. Casting began. Ethan Hawke signed on for the central role of Vincent (Jerome). He had this to say about the project:

Quote

> It's rare that you read a screenplay that has such an original voice to it. And this is a whole new take on the science fiction thriller....The environment Andrew creates is fascinating – it goes along with the theory that as the technology increases, so does isolation.

Uma Thurman accepted the role of Irene, attracted by the ideas built into the film, and the relationship between Irene and Vincent. Jude Law, then an unknown, was selected for the part of Jerome (Eugene), and the script changed to make his character English. Veteran actors Alan Arkin and Ernest Borgnine signed on as Detective Hugo and Caesar, and famous writer (and sometime actor) Gore Vidal as Director Josef. Celebrated European cinematographer Slawomir Idziak (*Blue* and other films) was engaged to direct photography, and British composer Michael Nyman (*The Piano* and other films) to score the film.

Niccol, working on a limited budget ($16,000,000), had to make creative adaptations in bringing his vision of the future to the screen. He did not have the luxury of creating a completely artificial world (like *Blade Runner*) or using state of the art special effects (as in *AI*). This however suited the cool, intellectual quality of the film. The main location chosen was the Marin County Civic Centre north of San Francisco. Niccol comments that it is 'slightly heroic in its architecture. We chose it also because it was from a period when people were optimistic about the future'. Niccol and cinematographer Idziak used lens filters routinely for outdoor scenes, creating what he alternatively describes as a 'jaundiced look' and/or a 'golden look' – a contradiction that well sums up the two ways of seeing such a technically 'perfect' but inhumane, arid future.

The movie went into production, and was released in 1997. It met with mainly enthusiastic reviews, though it was not a box office hit. It was nominated for an Academy Award (Best Art Direction-Set Decoration Jan Roelfs, Nancy Nye), a Golden Globe Award (Best Original Score Michael Nyman), an Apex Award (Action/Mystery/Thriller), a Golden Brando Award (Best Picture), a Golden Globes Award (*Best Original Score*), the Hugo Award, the Paris Film Festival prize and many others. It received the Best Film Award at the Catalonian International Film Festival (Spain), two prizes at the Gérardmer Film Festival (France), and Niccol was awarded Screenwriter of the Year (1999) at the London Film Critics Circle Awards.

Notes on Genre, Structure and Style

Genre

Gattaca is obviously a science fiction story. The key premise, of genetically selected babies ('vitros' or 'made men') growing up to dominate a society ruled by 'genoism' (genetic discrimination), is a classic example of the way 'speculative fiction' pushes an important and disturbing idea to its logical conclusion.

Serious science fiction movies

Although science fiction movies have often been dismissed as implausible entertainments, either high-tech variants of action thrillers (think of the *Star Wars* or *Terminator* series) or of horror films (think of *The Fly* or *Alien*), in fact there is an illustrious pedigree of serious SF films. If we think of *Forbidden Planet* (1956), in which Shakespeare's *The Tempest* was adapted to an off-world setting, *2001: A Space Odyssey* (1969), Kubrick's classic investigation of human identity, *Blade Runner* (1982), Ridley Scott's famous portrait of a future dystopia with artificial humans, *Artificial Intelligence* (1999), Spielberg's exploration of the same theme, and others – we see that the genre can be used to make quite insightful and moving comments on the nature of the world and of human potential.

Gattaca as 'prophetic realism'

One critic called SF 'prophetic realism', which is certainly a useful definition of the serious examples. In effect, the film maker starts with a prophecy – such as asserting that given the ability to manipulate genes, we will try to create a society of 'perfect people' – and then creates a story out of the proposition. Once the prophetic scenario is in place, everything else in the story proceeds in a 'normal' (ie realistic) fashion. Beyond accepting the initial premise, we are not asked to believe anything else that is implausible, and thereafter the movie proceeds according to standard narrative or genre-based rules. This explains *Gattaca* quite well. Its principal interest is in exploring the consequences of a troubling idea – human genetic 'engineering' on a massive scale – and it does so in a way that is both thoughtful and dramatic.

Gattaca as a mystery

However, it is more. It is also a detective or 'whodunnit' or mystery film, and to some extent a rather intellectual thriller. Let's consider these briefly.

Detective films start with a crime, and then follow the ensuing investigation. The most intriguing narratives have a mystery which

7

is not resolved easily. *Gattaca* follows this 'narrative tease' convention. The murder of the director is revealed as early as Scene 5. Then however we are taken on a massive flashback digression (Scenes 6-30). Only after we have returned to the 'present' of the film can the investigation begin. This occupies much of the rest of the film (Scenes 31-33, 35-37, 40, 43-47, 49-51, 53, 56-59, 61-62, 66-75, and 77 are explicitly about the investigation), a total of 33 scenes. Those that aren't following the detectives often concern the reactions of Vincent and Jerome (Eugene) to the investigation. So a large part of the film is concerned with this 'whodunnit' narrative thread.

Gattaca as a thriller

Although *Gattaca* is not a thriller in quite the sense of a Bruce Willis action adventure, it does have the built in tension, from the very first scene, of the 'will he be caught?' problem. The central character is living a false identity, and we don't know until Scene 84 (out of 88) whether he will pull off the deception.

Gattaca belongs to that rather small sub-group of thrillers in which the protagonist (or hero) courts disaster by *breaking the law*. Normally the hero is an obvious 'good guy' who is combating evil. Here Vincent is ostensibly doing the 'wrong' thing. However, Niccol positions us very carefully, making out a compelling argument that Vincent is right in his basic human instincts (wanting to succeed), and suggesting that it is the society which is wrong in trying to repress people like him with its 'genoism'. See for example Scene 15, in which our shock at how unfair the rejection is carries enormous weight and underpins this argument. The challenge of asking viewers to identify with a 'lawbreaker ' is treated with great delicacy. In case it should destabilise the film's 'message', Niccol finds ways of 'endorsing' Vincent's illegal scheme: Jerome (Eugene), Irene, Anton (finally) and most notably Doctor Lamar (Scene 84) all support him in his 'rebellion'. That the last mentioned is only shown to be a secret accomplice at the eleventh hour, and when it looks like he will be the obstacle to Vincent's triumph, is another 'thriller' trick, and it works very well.

Drama as a vehicle for serious themes

The question arises: why devote so many scenes to 'genre' trickery (deception, investigation, suspense, surprise revelations)? The answer is – that it drives the story. A good science fiction idea (what might happen in a future society) has little or no narrative energy in its own right. If however it is embedded in another type of narrative (here a detective thriller), the audience remains interested, and the subtextual development of the main idea (is such a society going the right way, or not?) can proceed at the same time. If you like, the detective plot is the vehicle which moves the story along, while the 'debate' about genetics etc is the intellectual content of the story. All serious SF movies do the same thing. We can stand back from a film like *Blade Runner* and discuss its take on human identity, or from *AI* and talk about whether artificial people are a good thing, but it is the *drama* of the movies that 'hooks' us and keeps us watching.

Gattaca is also of course a romance, or love story. The Vincent-Irene story occupies a significant number of scenes (2, 5, 35-36, 45, 48, 52-55, 61-65, 75-76, 81-2), easily a quarter of the film. It works on two levels. At a raw emotional level, it has great narrative power. Everyone loves a love story, and this one is no exception. We are pleased to see the hero get the girl. It is part of his triumph over the odds, his reward, as it were, for striving so heroically.

But something else is going on too. For the love story intersects with the film's major thematic subtext. Irene is imperfect and doesn't think she's good enough for a '9.3' (alpha male), despite the fact that we are invited, as viewers, to recognise her obvious good looks and appeal. He accepts her, regardless, thereby affirming the point Niccol is making about people's *innate* worth (as opposed to some outward or scientific measure). Then, ironically, the situation is reversed. *He* is revealed to be imperfect – indeed an 'In-valid'. By this time in the film, needless to say, our identification with him is complete, and it is no problem for us. But for the character of Irene? She accepts him, symbolically dropping the hair (which could be used for DNA analysis) in an echo of the way he dropped her hair, thereby making exactly the same thematic point (about people being valuable for *themselves*, not for how perfect they are).

So the love story, in alliance with the mystery/thriller story, leads us through the film. Both elements however carry their subtextual messages about the social issues which are Niccol's real concern.

Structure

Structurally, as suggested above, *Gattaca* has two major intersecting narrative structures – the mystery/thriller (which itself breaks down into two sub-sections – Vincent's deception and the murder investigation), and the romance. Added to this is the long flashback sequence, which takes us from Vincent's childhood through to his acceptance at Gattaca as the pretend Jerome

Gattaca as a romance

Subtext of the romance

Sub-plots

Morrow. Such narrative complexities make some demands on the audience, and need co-ordinating – the reason for the voice overs (see below under film technique).

Motifs

Niccol also likes motifs and repeated patterns. Motifs are recurrent visual or sound cues which come to have thematic meaning. Consider the number of shots in which Vincent cleans himself, or shaves, or sloughs off skin. There are repeated shots of urine and blood samples. There are the hair scenes (3, 35-36, 45, 63 and 81). They all underline the theme of the body as the identifier (and betrayer) in this society. There are the water scenes, (particularly 12, 16 and 80), moments of struggle and triumph over nature (represented at a subliminal level by the sea).

Doubles

Even more interesting is the way Niccol *doubles* characters. Vincent and Eugene are the obvious double, but so too are Vincent and Anton. What's going on here? Probably the idea that despite apparent differences (Vincent's imperfection, Anton's perfection) they are really equally 'valid' as human beings. And have you noticed the number of detectives in the film: Detective Hugo, the Investigator (Anton) and all the police glimpsed in the background, obviously, but also Irene, Doctor Lavar and even perhaps Caesar. This 'ups the ante' in terms of the movie's feeling of paranoia. It also argues that in a community founded on genetic engineering, detection and classification become pervasive, obsessive.

Style

Retro look

Stylistically, *Gattaca* is unusual. Although a case can be made that it has a dystopic (bleak or anti-idealistic) vision, the film conveys its criticism in a subdued way. *Gattaca's* 'retro' look draws on the Cold War iconography of the 50s. There are images of totalitarianism and allusions to Nazi war images. The sets also carry impressions of sterility. The main setting for the film is quite coldly scientific. The large spaces are uncluttered and well-lit. It is cavernous and devoid of much color.

For more detail on the film's style, see the cinematic notes which follow.

Reading a Film as Text

Actors and acting/characterisation

Performers always bring the story to life in ways which colour our response. We are used to the convention that the actors *are* the characters: we suspend our disbelief, forgetting that they are players on a set, and feel for them as the 'real' people they are playing. In this context, it is important to consider for a moment how well they animate their roles.

Ethan Hawke

Ethan Hawke, well known for his brooding, angst-ridden characters (*Dead Poet's Society*, *Great Expectations*, *Snow Falling on Cedars*) brings to the part of Vincent an inwardness which is interesting. There is a certain vulnerability, even frailty, to his portrayal, which well expresses the idea of a character who is physically weak, but determined to overcome his weakness. A square-jawed action hero might have subverted the film's far more intellectual tone and made the triumph of Vincent seem too easy.

Uma Thurman

Uma Thurman has played a range of parts, from the comic mobster girl in *Pulp Fiction*, to romantic leads (*The Truth about Cats and Dogs*), and even action heroes (*The Avengers*). But she has model good looks, a 'classical' style of speech and movement, and a quality of aloofness which well suits the part of Irene. Dressed as she is in the elegant but 50s retro clothes, with tightly coiffed hair, she comes across as the sort of 'ice maiden' you might expect in a controlled society like Gattaca. Seeing her 'let her hair down', as she does in Scenes 48, 55 and 62-3, is both a visual pleasure, and suggests the sort of 'awakening' or rebellion against conformity which the film implicitly recommends.

Jude Law

Jude Law was an unknown British actor when this film was made. He has since leaped to prominence, with films like *The Talented Mr Ripley*, *Enemy and the Gates*, *AI* (in which he is a mesmerising artificial human) and others. His range is wide, but he is remarkable for an inner 'fire', which is expressed in his intense gaze. Niccol chose him partly for 'the right level of superiority in his voice' and for his classical, 'perfect' looks. Law gives the character of Eugene not only an arrogance which fits with the idea of an Alpha class super-being, but also a sense of anger and frustration (at failing himself in a society predicated on the importance of being Number 1).

Other actors   Veteran actor Alan Arkin makes Hugo something of a stereotype of the 'hard-boiled' gumshoe, which suits the genre aspects of the movie very well. The hat and trenchcoat are a nod to the old Humphrey Bogart films of the genre. Loren Dean brings a quiet, controlled quality to the part of Anton/Investigator, ambiguous enough to put us off the scent about his real identity until the revelation scene (79). Gore Vidal, as the director, brings a quality of superior inscrutability to the role of the man who we least suspect, but who really 'dunnit' after all.

Mise en Scène

This film study term is French. It means 'scene setting', and refers to the design and visual elements of the movie, which, together with everything else on screen, are coded with meanings.

Sets and locations

Overall the film is visually austere and uncluttered, with a strong realist feel. It does not derive its art direction from either the comic book or the science fantasy tradition of science fiction. This is not SF with monsters or aliens, but 'prophetic neo-realism', dominated by people and symbolic locations.

It uses only ten different sets/locations, and the main ones (the Gattaca complex, the navigation lab, the space centre, Jerome's apartment, Irene's house, the police centre) are all bare, functional spaces. Smooth polished floors, bare walls, glass, vast airy interiors,
Modernist look   provide an overall atmosphere of modernism and minimalism. This encodes the idea of a society based on the principles of 'perfection' and scientific materialism. If we think of a very different science fiction mise en scène, like the smoggy, rainy exteriors and cluttered, crumbling interiors of *Blade Runner*, which portrays a nightmare future, we see how much 'restraint' has been built into *Gattaca's* 'look'.

The film had a relatively modest budget, and Niccol was not able
Locations   to create his own grand sets. He chose therefore to use locations with the right feel. Principal among these was the Frank Lloyd Wright building at Marin County (Gattaca). With its vast architectural scale, its futuristic yet 50s look, it was ideal for a film set in 'the not too distant future'.

The apartment   Eugene's/Jerome's apartment is another good example of the
as an example   'modernist' style. The circular staircase is inspired, and evokes

a number of connotations. It is a rather grand architectural feature, and suggests wealth and taste. It is also a textual allusion to Hitchcock films and thus to Hitchcock suspense. Thirdly, and most significantly, it has the shape of a double helix (the DNA pattern). When it is in the frame, the theme of genetics is thereby continually foregrounded.

'Scientific' mise en scène

The dominant mise en scène is one of huge spaces, shiny floors, glass, chrome, light – in short of science. Although there are sequences in a laboratory, there is little scientific 'content' or apparatus shown in the film. The principal items are the computer, the printer and the projection screen. There is no emphasis on gadgetry.

Lighting and colour

The 'palette' of the film is primarily green and blue/grey. Often the film approximates sepia. It is visually a 'cold' film. This is deliberate. Niccol and his cinematographer were at pains to establish the idea of a society that, in its desire to be 'perfect', has squeezed all humanity out. It has become as sterile as a laboratory.

Green filters

There are floods of green in the film (Niccol and Idziak used lens filters all the time). The green is largely naturalistic, but on occasions has a more symbolic function, coding moments of threat and tension. Murky colours of brown and green contribute mood to the 'noir' sequences (the alleyway; the sequence with the agent when Vincent 'resorts to extreme measures'; the first shots of Eugene), which 'quote' the *film noir* thrillers of the 40s. *Noir* was the conventional style for films of paranoia and detection in the Hollywood studio era. *Noir* style lighting effects are best illustrated in the sequence when Irene and Vincent are hiding from the police after Vincent had fought a guard. Irene and Vincent are shot in a squashed two shot with shadows of a grill crossing both faces. The street sequence (alleyway) is consistently shot in this 'colour noir' style.

Gold filters

In contrast to this dark lighting are the several scenes bathed in golden light. We think of the first scene in which Vincent's ambition (of going to the stars) is revealed (5). There is also the first scene of Vincent and Irene's intimacy (45), and the mirror farm scene (55), the nightclub scene (61), the final reconciliation scene (81), in which the gold captures the intimacy and excitement of this relationship. In these scenes the film displays warmth, excitement and (for this film) visual richness.

Framing and camera angles

We use the terms 'long shot' (showing the whole scene at once), 'medium shot' (showing two or more people in some detail) and 'close up shot' (one or two faces or other detail). There are also extreme close ups, a relative rarity. *Gattaca* uses all of these to effect.

Long shots

Many of the scenes shot in and around Gattaca (the facility) use extreme long shots (think of Scenes 45 and 76), the camera so far from the human characters that they are tiny figures in the distance. As might be expected, this carries a thematic message. They appear as insignificant, dwarfed by the massive architectural mass of the buildings. Why? Because the whole point of the film is to decry a social order which suppresses individuality and difference, and rewards conformity and scientific perfection. Niccol also uses extreme 'depth of field' in many shots. This is where we see the foreground and the background equally well. Such shots give a feeling of space. Once again the point is that individuals are unimportant in this brave new world.

Medium shots

Extreme close-ups

Like most movies, *Gattaca* shows a majority of scenes in unselfconscious medium shots, and intimate scenes in close ups. But we should note in passing the director's bold use of extreme close ups. The very first scene is a dramatic example (fingernails, hairs, skin, in alarming close up). So too are the traitor eyelash shot (Scene 31), and the several scenes in which individual hairs are signficant (3, 35-36, 45, 63 and 81). These subliminally remind us of the film's premise: that in a society ruled by genes, the smallest body fragments can be ruinously important.

Framing

Framing also refers to how people or things are arranged inside the frame (the composition of shots). The shot showing Vincent squatting on the beach sloughing his skin after his night with Irene (64) is an example of significant framing. The camera captures him as if he were a Roman statue. This shot invests him with the dignity of the classic man (Roman sculpture, Michelangelo), while also reinforcing his vulnerability and the theme of body betrayal.

Think too of the shot which introduces us to Eugene. He is positioned on the right side of the frame (not centrally) and shot with side lighting. The light concentrates on his aggressive stare and his set chin as he radiates tension and hostility. This introduction is all the more forceful because of the lack of dialogue. In the first four shots of Eugene in this sequence, he says nothing. Jude Law holds his body with steely rigidity. The first words Eugene says are in response to Vincent's question about who lives up there? Eugene spits out 'Well I certainly don't'.

The sea shots   The sea sequences are highly charged. The underwater scenes seem to be acting as womb/birth images. The boys are attracted to the sea as the site for competition, and the film has clearly differentiated between the circumstances of their conception and genetic makeup. The camera on occasions is under the water, at other times allowing a god's eye view of the boys swimming. The images of the water and the boys' struggles in the water appear to have a birth component about them. Of course the darkness of some of the shots also suggests danger and fear of drowning.

Editing

Editing (or 'cutting') is the device by which different shots are joined to make a meaningful sequence. All films use it, necessarily. What is connected with what is of course extremely important, and it is a standard of 'film grammar' to make associations by cutting.

Fast (dramatic)   This technique is probably seen at its most interesting in the
'cutting'   highly dramatic scenes – such as the gymnasium scene (44) in which Vincent nearly gives himself away, in the road tunnel scene (53) in which he is nearly caught by the police, and the nightclub and alley scenes (61-2), when he narrowly avoids capture. The technique of building and sustaining suspense is also seen to good effect in the series of scenes centring on the Jerome/Eugene substitution (69-75), in which we have different locations (car, apartment, roadside, apartment) in successive scenes, building up to the climactic moment when Eugene, despite his handicap, pulls off a show of normality for the investigator.

Scene 'doubling'   We should not leave this topic without reference to the final scenes. Here, the ascent of Vincent into space is intercut with Eugene's suicide, probably the most challenging parallel in the film. The doubling is intensified by the enclosure (capsule, incinerator), the lighting (stark), the motif of fire, and the linking voice over. What these scenes, and the editing, do is bond the two men, and show their mutual fulfilment (one in going 'up there', the other in the long awaited rest of death).

Sound

Title sequence sounds

Gattaca uses sound in an interesting way, employing all the standard techniques to advance its meaning.

We have only to look at the precredit sequence to see the skill with which Niccol manipulates us. The close-ups (of hairs and skin) give the spectator ambiguous visual information, arousing curiosity (what are these things?). Meanwhile, the soundtrack matches the falling objects with booming sounds. When it becomes clear that we are watching hairs falling, the disjunction between vision and sound jars. Only at a microscopic level could hairs 'crash' like trees. Yet this disjunction points up a key theme of the film: the importance of body parts in a world dedicated to genetic perfection.

Voice over

Dialogue is extremely important in this film. Key themes are foregrounded in speeches. It is quite a 'literary' film. *Gattaca* also uses 'voice over' narration – a relatively rare device – in the flashback sequence (Scenes 6-30) and in the final scenes (85-88). This is essential, because it clarifies and co-ordinates the narrative. Huge time jumps are involved, linked only by the voice over track. In the flashback, vital information (why Vincent had a problem, how he reacted, how he developed his daring scheme, how the scheme was executed, etc) is communicated in a speedy way. To have shown this in conventional form, with scenes of dialogue explaining what was going on, would have extended the film considerably, and lessened the drama. The voice over also allows the director to play interesting games with the audience. The confessional voice tells all about Jerome Morrow and then drops the bombshell: 'I am *not* Jerome Morrow'.

Music

Music plays a key part in the film too. Veteran film composer Michael Nyman provided the music track. The orchestral music sets a tone of sombre reflectiveness, and moments of drama to match the thriller aspects of the story. The piano solo (Scenes 48 & 52) is haunting and, once we find out about the six fingers, pregnant with meaning. This is reprised towards the end of the film.

SFX

Sound effects (SFX) are another feature of the movie. We have already noted the amazing falling hairs effect (Scene 1). Think too of the sound of the cars in the road crossing sequence – a dramatic and significant scene. As spectators we are asked to experience Vincent's fear as he crosses the busy freeway unable to see the cars. This sequence is shot shot out of focus as a subjective shot – the vision matching the sound – to capture Vincent's myopia and the danger he is in.

Summary and Commentary

Scene 1 - Title Sequence

Supers

The film opens with a black screen, on which we read the title, **'Consider God's handiwork; who can straighten what He hath made crooked?'** (Ecclesiastes) **'I not only think that we will tamper with Mother Nature. I think Mother wants us to.'** (Wittgenstein)

Falling objects

A blue screen appears. Giant translucent arcs are falling onto a flat surface, making booming noises. Tree-like objects crash onto the surface. As the title (*Gattaca*) comes up, what appears to be snow is falling – then black fragments. These resolve themselves gradually into what seem to be human hairs. Then flakes make a matting on the surface. Hairs, flakes, and then we cut to a razor scraping hairs off a man's chin.

Boldily preparations

We see a young man ('Jerome') shaving. We see him sloughing his skin with a brush and pumice stone – his arms, his legs, and his chest – and brushing his hair. He showers in an enclosed cubicle. He leaves the cubicle, closes the door and flames burst into life, incinerating and cleaning the inside.

He reaches into a fridge and takes out a transparent suspension bag filled with what appears to be urine, which he straps around his thigh. He injects blood into a hollow flesh coloured capsule. We see him at a workbench. The flesh-coloured capsule is a fingertip pad which he is gluing onto his finger.

We see the outside of a stark modern building, and a car driving away. We see another modern building as the title sequences end.

Commentary The opening images of *Gattaca* announce its fictional premise in a way that is both artistic and intellectually challenging. The mystery of the falling objects – a clever 'come on' in itself – is resolved as we see that we are looking at debris from the human body, magnified to such an extent that a human hair is like a tree trunk. This focusses our attention on what is to be the argument of the film: that in a hypothetical future society, we are defined by the very cells in our body. (The argument will be given its full exposition in flashback scenes 6-15.) The ominous 'boom' of the falling hairs (and other fragments) underlines the importance of the body. The apparent anxiety of the young man, sloughing off skin and hair, points us towards the drama which will unfold (concerning his fake identity). This connects with the fake urine sample, prompting the question (in the viewer's mind): what is he up to? The flames of the cleansing cubicle anticipate the end of Jerome (Eugene) – of which more later.

Finally, after the somewhat claustrophobic close-ups and interiors of the opening shots, we see an exterior. It has a bare, futuristic look about it. The car glides with an electronic whirr. A strange yellow filter gives the whole scene an eerie light. We are subliminally put on notice that the world of *Gattaca* is a strange, troubling place – apparently orderly and sterile – in fact claustrophic and totalitarian.

Scene 2: Gattaca aeronautical facility, interior, day

Gattaca

The young man we have seen (Jerome) is entering the facility. He does a finger print test and the green light flashes, as we see the title **'The not too distant future'**. This is followed by a pin-prick blood test. He is followed by a blond girl (Irene). She looks at him, curiously. They enter the facility.

Scene 3: Flight training centre, day

Jerome is working at a computer, navigating a flight simulator. When he has successfully completed the exercise, he uses a miniature vacuum cleaner to suck up body debris on the keyboard.

Jerome's mission

The assistant director of the facility comes down the aisle and stops at Jerome's place. The director complimentshim on his **cleanliness**. Coolly, Jerome replies, **'It's next to godliness'**. The director compliments him on his perfect score (on the flight simulator), and refers to the coming flight to Titan – in a week's time. The director moves away. Surreptiously, Jerome pulls out a file containing skin dust, which he shakes over the keyboard. He puts a hair on a comb and carefully inserts it into the desk.

Scene 4: Gattaca medical centre

The doctor (Lamar) hands Jerome a plastic vial for a urine sample. As Jerome urinates, the doctor watches and comments admiringly on his 'great piece of equipment', wishing that *his* parents had

Jerome's 'valid identity'

ordered the same. The doctor puts the urine sample into a tester. On the screen, we see a picture of a person vaguely like Jerome and the name **'Morrow, Jerome'** and below, **'Valid'**. The doctor asks Jerome how he feels about the coming voyage and why he is not excited. Jerome tells him he will reply at the end of the week.

Scene 5: Inside the Gattaca centre, day

Irene

Jerome is watching the launch of a rocket. Irene joins him. She tells him, **'If you are going to pretend not to be excited, don't watch every launch'**.

A voice over (Jerome's) tells us that he is a Navigator (First Class) due to fly on a one-year voyage to Titan. This was almost *The truth about* predestined, because of his perfect 'genetic quotient'. The only *Jerome (Vincent)* problem, he adds, is that '**I am *not* Jerome**'.

(While this voice over has been going on, Jerome has moved inside the facility. A crowd has gathered by what appears to be a pool of blood near a doorway.)

Commentary These scenes resolve the question of why Jerome (Vincent) has fake urine and blood samples. He is an imposter. The reason is not yet clear, but the peril of his situation is subtly underlined. He is watchful, guarded, and forced to remove all traces of his real identity (the body samples which accidentally fall on the keyboard), and to substitute bogus ones. The moment when Irene catches him watching the rocket blast off is clearly a significant one. She has noticed something which he has tried to conceal – not his fake identity (yet) but his carefully staged air of indifference to the launches. He is obviously a man with a secret, and therefore highly vulnerable.

Just as Scene 5 ends, the first sign of a greater emergency appears – the murder (of the director). No details are given, and the film now embarks on a lengthy digression (about Vincent's past, real identity and secret scheme), but viewers cannot fail to see that some sort of crisis has intervened to further threaten this young man's precarious deceit.

Scene 6: Beachfront, Detroit (flashback)

Vincent's conception

A car is parked by the beachfront. In the back seat are a couple. Jerome's voice over explains that he was conceived on the Detroit 'Riviera'. He says:

They used to say that a child conceived in love has a greater chance of happiness. They don't say that anymore.

Scene 7: A labour ward, hospital, day (flashback)

Vincent's birth

Vincent's mother has just given birth. The nurse carries the baby away from her and administers a simple pinprick blood test to the tiny foot. The drop of blood is then scanned genetically.

Ten fingers, ten toes, that's all that used to matter. Not now. Now, only seconds old, the exact time and cause of my death was already known.

Vincent's DNA profile and life predictions

Mother affirms his potential

A computer printout is read aloud by the nurse, detailing the genetic predispositions of the baby. They include a 99% chance of heart disease, and a life expectancy of just over 30 years. Vincent's father, watching and listening, is totally unnerved. A nurse asks what name the baby will have. The mother says 'Anton' (after the father), but the father says 'Vincent Anton'. He doesn't want an imperfect child to have his name. The mother however, now holding the baby again, says, **'I know you will be something!'**

Scene 8: Vincent's house, exterior, day (flashback)

Childhood problems

Young Vincent runs and falls over. His mother anxiously hurries out and picks him up, cuddling him. The voice-over explains that every accident and danger he was exposed to was a cause for concern.

Scene 9: Kindergarten (flashback)

The kindergarten director will not allow Vincent to be admitted because of insurance problems. She closes the gate against the parents.

Scene 10 – Geneticist's office (flashback)

Vincent's parents enter the office and sit down. Young Vincent is with them. On the computer screen are the images of four fertilized eggs. They have come to provide Vincent with a little brother. The

Engineering a brother

geneticist explains that the mother's eggs have been fertilized with the father's sperm. After eliminating those showing any genetic predisposition to medical or other problems, only four fertilized eggs are left. He invites the parents to choose. The parents express preference for a boy, a brother for Vincent. The parents are a little uneasy about the degree of selection and intervention involved. **'We were just considering if it's good to just leave a few things to chance.'** The geneticist replies,

Quote

You want to give your child the best possible start. Believe me we have enough imperfections built in already...Keep in mind this child is still you. Simply the best of you.

Scene 11: Vincent's home, interior, day (flashback)

Anton: the perfect specimen

The father is measuring Anton's height. Forlornly, young Vincent, now a boy of ten wearing glasses, sees that his own height is considerably below that of his genetically perfect brother. He rubs off the mark indicating his own height.

Scene 12: Seaside, daytime (flashback)

Young Anton and young Vincent run across the sand dunes and stop near the sea. Vincent's voice-over says that by *that* time he understood there was something very different flowing through Anton's veins to that flowing through his. **'And I'd need an awful lot more than a drop if I was going to get anywhere.'** Young Vincent uses a sharp shell to cut his thumb, drawing blood. He hands the shell to Anton, but Anton is unable to cut his skin.

Vincent's defeat

Vincent's voice-over explains that their favourite game was 'chicken'. They would swim out into the sea as far as they could, waiting to see who would give up first. We watch them swimming out to sea, struggling through the water. Vincent gives up first, because Anton is far stronger.

Scene 13 – Car park, day (flashback)

We start on a close-up of a red ball (representing the sun). As the camera rises, we see the planets of the solar system laid out at carefully staged intervals to represent the size of the system.

Vincent's dream – going into space

Vincent's voice-over explains that his growing reluctance for this planet translated into an interest for others, and he had **'dreamed of going into space'**. They reach the end planet (Pluto). Anton picks up the apple representing the planet and is about to eat it, but Vincent grabs the apple back. Anton is proclaiming that he could go into space if he wanted to.

Scene 14 – Vincent's home, day (flashback)

The lack of hope in Vincent's life

The whole family are eating. Vincent is looking at a book on space careers. His mother tries to dissuade him from an interest in such things, reminding him of his potential heart condition. He declares that it's only a one percent chance. His father gets involved, and says: **'Look, the only way you will see the inside of a spaceship is if you're cleaning it.'**

Scene 15 – Gattaca facility, interview centre, day (flashback)

Vincent's defeat

Vincent is waiting with a number of other men for an interview. His voice-over, explains that genetic testing is used for all interviews. Though discrimination is officially illegal, no one takes any notice of that. Testing is commonplace. In the interview room, young Vincent shakes hands with the interviewer (as his voice-over comments, they take samples from handshakes, or the saliva on a letter). The interviewer places a plastic beaker (for a urine sample) before Vincent. Reluctantly, Vincent leaves the room.

Commentary These scenes lay out the speculative premise of the film. In a future world dedicated to 'perfection' through genetic selection, people like Vincent, who was born naturally (and is therefore imperfect), are part of a disadvantaged minority. The contrast is underlined dramatically in the difference between Vincent and his perfect brother Anton. In abandoning Nature in favour of Science, people (in this brave new world) have achieved what they thought they wanted – the ideal human being – free of defects. But what appears at first to be so admirable (**'You want to give your child the best possible chance'** and **'this child is still you. Simply the best of you'**) they have also moved towards what the film will call **'genoism'** (prejudice based on genetic profile).

In focussing our attention so clearly on the predicament of Vincent, who has no future because of his genetic profile, the filmmaker engages our sympathy for him, and implicitly positions us to despise the social policies which have created his unhappiness. Through no fault of his own, and against the appearance of absolute normality, he is trapped in a form of hell. Anton's arrogance, his father's callous remark and the crushing defeat in the interview room all reinforce our empathy for his despair. This is important, because it sets up our understanding of why he takes the extreme measures to break out of his destiny (Scenes 16-30), which follow.

Scene 16: Beach, daytime (flashback)

The pivotal change in Vincent

Young Anton and Vincent are standing looking at the sea. Anton warns Vincent that he will lose again. The boys run into the sea and swim out, as previously. This day however is different. Vincent (in voice-over) explains that he was right there behind Anton all the way. Finally Anton gives up, calling out desperately out to his brother. Anton is exhausted and sinking beneath the water. Vincent returns and grabs him, dragging him back towards the beach. Vincent pulls Anton up onto the seashore.

Quote

It was the one moment in our lives that my brother was not as strong as he believed, and I was not as weak. It was the moment that made everything else possible.

Commentary This scene is the lynch pin of the film. It is the middle one of three scenes dedicated to the swimming challenges between Vincent and Anton. The first one (Scene 12) shows Vincent defeated. The last one (Scene 80) is practically at the end of the film, and not known to us at this point, but will show him triumphant. This one is the key turning point in the story. Having previously accepted what he takes to be the 'fact' of his 'inferiority', Vincent now challenges it. The swimming race is symbolic of his newfound determination to beat his destiny. By what we understand to be a triumph of willpower, he pushes Anton to his limit, and swaps places, taking over as the dominant brother. His saving of Anton (from drowning) shows that this has nothing to do with simpleminded aggression or oneupmanship – it is his own personal discovery that motivation and attitude are key determinants in human experience, not just genetics and expectation. This idea is to be the central argument of the whole film. Niccol signals the idea first in what is a physical context (a race), but the voice over points us towards the far more pervasive implications of Vincent's realisation. The dramatic climax of the race (and near drowning) serve to underline the ideological climax (and reversal) which is the real point of this scene.

Scene 17: Vincent's home, day (flashback)

Vincent is looking at a family photograph. He rips out the corner of the picture which contains his head. He is leaving home, watched by Anton.

Scene 18: Gattaca centre, exterior, day (flashback)

Vincent's apparent destiny

A vehicle drives up loaded with young men in janitors' uniforms. The voice-over tells us that Vincent travelled, joining the 'new underclass' of the genetically inferior. **'We now have discrimination down to a science'**. Vincent looks up and sees a rocket launch. The supervisor (Caesar), asks him if he is '**dreaming of space**', gives him a bucket and mop and tells him to clean 'that space'. Vincent continues to watch the launches.

Scene 19: Gattaca centre, interior, night (flashback)

Thoughts of rebellion

Vincent is polishing the floor. He stops at one of the navigator's desks and tries out the idea of being one of the elite. At that moment, Caesar comes in, and he returns to polishing the floor.

Scene 20: Gattaca centre, interior, day (flashback)

Vincent is looking through the glass window at the Gattaca staff. Caesar warns him that he 'might get ideas'. He replies that he is cleaning the glass in order to make it easier for the supervisor to see him when he is inside.

Scene 21: Gattaca, bowling alley, night (flashback)

A plan suggests itself

Vincent is tidying up. He finds a mysterious implement (a heartrate monitor), which he pockets thoughtfully. At the check-in area (where the blood tests are taken automatically) he puts his finger on the testing surface, and feels the pinprick. The red light is flashing, indicating that he is 'In-valid'.

Scene 22 – Vincent's apartment, day (flashback)

Rebellion

Vincent is hanging upside down, doing sit ups, with a heavy celestial navigation volume as a weight. He drops to the floor, exhausted. His voice-over reveals that no amount of conditioning will help him without the right blood type. '**I made up my mind to resort to more extreme measures.**' Vincent is looking at a light bulb (representing the sun) around which circle planets.

Later, in his apartment, the black market gene broker (German) appears. He measures Vincent. German opens a case and pulls out a vial of blood. Vincent holds it up and looks at it.

Commentary In these scenes, Vincent is working through the implications of his new determination to beat his destiny. He has used his lowly status as a janitor to get inside Gattaca. A plan is forming (represented by picking up the heart monitor), although it does not crystallise until Scene 22. His commitment to get to the stars (an ambition both literal and symbolic, when we think about it) remains firm. He has been training to beat his physical weaknesses. He is focussed on his goal (represented by the solar system model). But he realises that commitment and training are not enough. In a system which prejudges him on genetic grounds, he must play a more devious game. This is where the gene broker comes in. But will it be that easy?

Scene 23: Exterior of Jerome's apartment, day (flashback)

The fake identity scheme

Vincent and the gene broker are walking towards the apartment. Vincent's voice-over explains that even the genetically perfect sometimes suffer accidents. '**One man's loss is another man's gain,**' he adds.

Scene 24: Jerome's apartment, interior, day (flashback)

The broker explains in a whisper to Vincent that Jerome is a perfect specimen – in terms of IQ, longevity, and strength. The broker explains to Vincent that he was 'a big time swimming champion' until he broke his back. '**You could go everywhere, with this guy's helix tucked under your arm.**' At that moment Jerome appears, in a wheelchair. When he sees the two of them together, German claims that they are very much alike. Vincent disputes it. The broker dismisses Vincent's concerns, saying no one ever looks at photographs anyway. Vincent asks about the accident. German explains that the beauty of the situation is that it happened out of the country, so for all intents and purposes Jerome is still a fully

Jerome: the
perfect
specimen

functioning member of society. '**Blood has no nationality. As long as its got what they're looking for, it's the only passport you need**.' While he is saying this, Jerome smoking icily, looks on. '**So began the process of becoming Jerome**,' concludes Vincent's voice over.

Scene 25: Jerome's apartment, night (flashback)

German is using eye-testing apparatus to establish what corrective contact lenses Vincent will need to become Jerome. We see a close up of hair shavings. The modifications continue. We see Vincent comparing himself to the photograph of the *real* Jerome.

Transformation of
Vincent into
'Jerome'

(Later) 'That's it', says Vincent with relief. German tells that there is just one other thing – the matter of the height difference. Only one modification is believable – and it involves surgery. Vincent refuses completely. Looking on, Jerome asks if he (Vincent) is 'really serious' (about his ambition).

We cut to a close up of a surgical saw.

We cut to Vincent lying flat out of the floor of the apartment, with surgical braces on his legs. The voice-over tells us that he endured the pain (after the operation) knowing that it would put him '**closer to the stars**'.

Commentary The counterfeiting of Jerome (Vincent) has proceeded according to plan. However, inevitably, there are challenges. And the moment when Vincent realises that to make the deceit work he will have to undergo painful surgery provokes a crisis. His initial reaction (thinking of the pain) is to give up. Interestingly, it is Eugene (the real Jerome) who pushes him back onto his plan.

I thought you were serious... [followed by:] Jerome never questioned my commitment again. I took my mind off the pain by reminding myself that when I eventually did stand up, I'd be exactly two inches closer to the stars.

This is another turning point, like Scene 16 (the swimming race won by Vincent). It again argues (at a level of subtext) that willpower and the courage to face pain and difficulty is an essential ingredient in success.

Scene 26: Jerome's apartment, day (flashback)

Doubts

Vincent is practising writing with his right hand. Jerome is collecting blood samples. He moves his wheelchair round and shows Vincent the medallion that he got for swimming. He points out that it was a silver medal. He adds, '**Jerome Morrow was never meant to be one step down....With all I had going for me, I was still second best. Me. So how do *you* expect to pull this off?**'

Scene 27: Exterior of Jerome's apartment, night (flashback)

Vincent's dream

Jerome in his wheelchair, and Vincent, on crutches, are looking across at the Gattaca centre. The voice-over tells us that Jerome had everything he needed to get into Gattaca, '**except the desire to do so**'. Jerome asks Vincent why he wants to get into there. Vincent replies that it is not the centre, but '**up there**' (the stars) he wishes to get to. Jerome tells Vincent that he should begin to call him Eugene and to start getting used himself to the name Jerome.

Scene 28: Jerome's apartment, day (flashback)

'Jerome' (Vincent) is dressed ready for the Gattaca interview. He needs a urine sample, which he collects from the fridge. He puts a drop onto the testing machine, but it registers as unacceptable. 'Eugene' (Jerome) has been drinking. Several times, Vincent tests urine samples, becoming more anxious – his interview is in an hour. Finally one tests as it should. He asks Eugene if he wants to pull out. Eugene is silent.

Scene 29: Gattaca testing centre (flashback)

Success of the substitution

The doctor tests the urine sample. On the screen the photograph and name are those of Jerome Morrow. The doctor congratulates Jerome (Vincent). He asks when the interview is. The doctor replies: '**That was it [the interview]**'.

Scene 30: Jerome's apartment, day (flashback)

Jerome (Vincent) appears at the top of the stairs. '**I got it**.' Eugene replies, '**Of course you got it**.'

The new Vincent – 'Jerome'

The scene fades to a series of images in the apartment – of Jerome sloughing off skin and removing hair, showering to disguise his true identity. All traces of his real self are incinerated in the cleansing cubicle. Eugene prepares samples of his own genetic code (urine, blood) so that Vincent (the *new* Jerome) can pass as him. The voice over compares the status of '**a valid, a vitro, a made man**' with his own.

Quote

I was now a member of a particularly detested segment of society. One of those who refuses to play the hand that he was dealt. I am most commonly known as a 'borrowed ladder' or a 'de-gene-erate'.

We see rows of shirts and other clothes in sealed plastic bags, and the label 'Confidentiality Guaranteed'.

Commentary The flashback is now over, its job of retrospective exposition done. We know why and how Vincent (Jerome) has assumed another man's identity. This is an interesting segment, as is the whole deceit subplot. When you think about it, why don't we take a conventional view of all this and condemn the illegality of what Vincent is doing? He is after all committing fraud. Yet we are not inclined to despise him, or to feel guilt by association. On the contrary, we are positioned to see what he has done as a triumph of determination. Our admiration for Vincent has been mightily enhanced in these scenes. Unlike the arrogant 'Valids' (Anton and Eugene), who were born perfect because of genetic engineering, but have done nothing to earn our respect, Vincent has worked himself up to be within striking distance of his dream by sheer courage. And he has beaten what are manifestly *unfair* odds. The terrible joke about the interview being a urine sample (Scene 29) brings home to us how cruelly discriminatory the Gattaca system is. 'Prejudice' is not mentioned anywhere in the film, but it is implicit everywhere. Niccol has shown us, as we feel for Vincent, what it means, and has urged us to support him in his subversion of it.

Two other stimulating ideas related to the movie's ideological subtext (or argument) appear in these scenes. One is mention of '**the burden of perfection**' – Eugene's problem. The other is the telling line: '**Jerome [Eugene] had been engineered with everything he needed to get into Gattaca except [for] the desire to do so**'. Niccol is surely making out a very powerful case here that genes are *not* the key issue. (Physical) perfection can be a 'burden', since it robs an individual of the challenge to rise above his or her potential. And 'desire' (or will, or motivation) is what really makes the difference – not genes.

Scene 31: Gattaca, interior, day

The murder – and its threat to Vincent

We are back in the dramatic 'present' of the film. Jerome (Vincent) rubs his eye, looking anxiously at the pool of blood spreading out into the hallway. He joins the crowd surrounding the body of the director. We see a close up of Jerome's eyelash, and the voice over says, '**He [the director] may have more success exposing me in death than he ever did in life**'.

Scene 32: Gattaca, interior, day

We see a keyboard, covered with blood. The detective (Hugo) says ironically, 'I think we can rule out suicide'.

Scene 33: Gattaca, interior, day

The detectives investigate, vacuuming and checking, watched by Jerome (Vincent).

The police investigation begins

(Later) the new director (Josef) takes Irene aside, asking her to help the investigators. She is reluctant, but he insists.

Jerome (Vincent) asks the director if this (the murder) will mean the mission being cancelled. The director replies, 'It hasn't stopped the planets turning'.

Jerome's eyelash is picked up.

Scene 34: Jerome's apartment, day

Vincent defiant

Defiantly, Jerome (Vincent) tells Eugene that he is 'going up' (regardless of the investigation). Eugene replies that they have to get drunk immediately.

Scene 35: Restaurant, night

Jerome (Vincent) wheels Eugene in.

Scene 36: Gattaca, interior, night

Irene checks Jerome (Vincent) Irene is going through Jerome's (Vincent's) drawer. She finds the hair that he has planted.

Scene 37: DNA centre, night

Irene hands in the specimen for analysis. The hair is tested. The attendant announces to Irene that it shows him to be '**9.3…Quite a catch!**' Irene examines the printout of Vincent's DNA.

Scene 38 – Restaurant, night

Jerome and Vincent share a drink. Eugene ponders the weightlessness of space. Eugene says:

> Quote

I can't believe you pulled this off. They're sending you up there….You, of all people!

Bond between Jerome (Vincent) and Eugene Jerome (Vincent) wants to know how Eugene will occupy himself while he is in space. Eugene will not reply, but drinks almost a full glass of wine at one draught. He asks about Titan. Jerome shows him by blowing smoke into a glass. Jerome tells him '**You should be going instead of me**', explaining '**up there your legs wouldn't matter**'. Eugene replies: '**I'm scared of heights**'.

Scene 39: Jerome's apartment, night

Outside, while Jerome plugs the car in for recharging, Eugene vomits. He jokes about saving power.

Jerome pushes Eugene inside in his wheelchair. We cut to the bedroom, and Jerome putting him, with difficulty, to bed. Eugene suddenly confesses that he wasn't drunk when he walked in front of the car that crippled him. He adds, '**If at first you don't succeed, try, try again!**' Suddenly, Eugene pulls Jerome down to him and says '**I'm proud of you Vincent!**'

Commentary After the flashback (scenes 6-30), the 'thriller' or murder mystery elements of the film become very concentrated. The narrative focus is on the investigation, and on the possibility of Vincent being exposed by it – probably not for the murder (though we haven't enough information yet to be sure), but certainly as an impostor. Throughout the rest of the movie, we are drawn along by the moves of the detectives, and Jerome and Eugene's attempts at evasion.

At the same time, curious things are emerging about two other characters who have up till now been secondary: Irene and Eugene.

It is interesting that Irene at this point in the story seems almost an enemy of Vincent, collecting evidence against him. This will turn out to be a false lead, but it adds for a time to the tension. Also, there is a mystery about her. Why has she singled out Jerome (Vincent)? Does she suspect him? Does she have a special interest in him? And why is she so downcast when she discovers that he is (apparently) a nearly perfect genetic specimen? We don't know – but it may be taken as pointing to some secret (yet to be revealed) of hers.

And what of the revelations about Eugene? First we have his conspicuous silence when asked what he will do while Jerome (Vincent) is in space. That, combined with him getting deliberately drunk, his confession about having already tried to kill himself, and his hint about doing it again (Scene 39) – set up an expectation (his eventual suicide) that adds another layer of drama to the story. On the positive side, however, we also see how far the two men's relationship has advanced – from the cold business arrangement of earlier scenes, through the shared challenge of the deception (and especially Eugene's role in pushing Jerome on), and into what is now a real intimacy. When Eugene pulls Jerome down, we almost expect a kiss. Instead, there is the understated but powerfully significant 'I'm proud of you, Vincent!' Eugene is using his real name, partly because he is drunk, but partly also because he is acknowledging the real hero (Vincent) behind the false identity (Jerome). In this, we sense the filmmaker using another character to signpost his own view of the protagonist – the hero of the story.

Scene 40: Police centre, night

Vincent identified

Officers are examining the dead director's body and taking samples from the crushed skull. One such sample is analysed genetically. On the screen we see Vincent, and the word 'In-valid'. The chief investigator is startled as he sees this.

Scene 41: Jerome's apartment, night

Eugene is exercising. Jerome takes the heart monitor from him.

Scene 42: Gattaca gymnasium, day

A new danger

Gattaca personnel are all exercising, their fitness levels being monitored. Jerome (Vincent) comes in and walks to a treadmill. He swaps the heart monitor (to the one he brought from the apartment). Irene watches him.

Scene 43: Gattaca centre, interior, day

Detective Hugo is telling his boss (the chief investigator) that they have found their man (Vincent). The investigator is sceptical. Hugo is going to check the suspect's family, but the investigator tells him that he has already done that and that there are no living relatives. Hugo is not convinced, but is silenced by his boss's look.

Scene 44: Gattaca centre, day

Dr Lamar admires Jerome's perfect heartbeat. Hugo and the investigator enter and meet up with the director. telling him about the 'in-valid' suspect. The investigator asks whether any less than perfect specimens are taken on in Gattaca. '**No one exceeds his potential**,' the director tells him.

Vincent is nearly exposed

At this point, we cut to the gym, and Jerome (Vincent), looking ill. The amplified heartbeat suddenly goes out of control. Jerome rips off the monitor and rushes from the gym.

We see him in the locker room, collapsing with the effort of his exercise.

(Later) Jerome walks out again, apparently fine.

The investigator is talking to Irene, asking her for an alibi. She tells him she was alone (at the time of the director's death). He tells her he finds it hard to believe.

Jerome has a paper cup (with water). He stops on the stairs beside (Chief Janitor) Caesar, who says, 'I'll take care of that for you, Mr Morrow'.

Scene 45 – Gattaca, exterior, day

Irene is looking up at a rocket launch. Jerome (Vincent) approaches her.

Irene tells him that she has checked his genetic profile. She

adds, '**It seems you are everything they say you are, and more**'.
She then confesses to him that she has a slight heart defect,
sufficient to stop her going into space. Jerome tells her, '**if there's
anything wrong with you, I can't see it**'. She plucks a hair, and
gives it to him, (inviting him to have it analysed). He holds the hair
between his finger and thumb, and then drops it. 'I'm sorry, the
wind caught it,' he lies. They walk off together.

*Vincent affirms
Irene as she is*

Scene 46 – Gattaca, interior, day

*The threat
intensifies*

Jerome (Vincent) is at his console. The image of Vincent appears
on the screen alongside his navigation simulation. He looks around
anxiously. No one is taking any notice.

The director appears and points at the screen. To Jerome's relief,
he is just checking the flight path. Jerome and Irene exchange glances.

Scene 47 – Jerome's apartment, day

Eugene is on the phone complaining about being sent the wrong
hair dye. Jerome (Vincent) comes in, despondent. He tells Eugene
that his image is everywhere at Gattaca, and 'They'll recognise
me'. He begins to destroy the samples. Eugene, furious, intervenes.
He accuses Jerome of having no 'spine', and tells him he could
have chosen any number of people to give his identity to. He
assures Jerome that they believe that he *is* Jerome. Jerome hands
over the blood sample.

*Vincent
almost
gives up*

Later we see close up shots of Jerome sloughing his skin, and
trying to remove all hairs. He appears later dressed up, telling Eugene
that he is going out. Jerome doesn't want to not attend the party,
and appear suspicious. Eugene points to the glasses that he is
accidentally wearing. He removes them immediately. Outside, Irene
is waiting in a car. Eugene looks at her thoughtfully from the window.

Commentary The 'net' is closing around Jerome (Vincent) in these scenes,
which are highly suspenseful. First comes the official
identification of the 'In-valid' (Vincent) who had no right to be
inside Gattaca. This danger is pushed to breaking point when
Vincent's image appears on every screen in the facility. Next
there is the near failure of the deception at the fitness test, from
which Jerome only just escapes. Finally, there is the sighting by
Caesar, who is the only person able to recognise Vincent from
his old job (and identity). All these tests he passes.

Yet the stress produces another crisis of confidence, one from which he is rescued, again, by Eugene. It is the second time he has almost faltered in his resolve (the other being Scene 25). This is a useful counterpoint to what might otherwise have seemed like Vincent's indomitable (and perhaps unbelievable) heroism. He knows that he is 'hanging in there' by willpower alone, and is subject to fears like everyone. The key point is not that he he has fears, but that he is capable of surviving them, and returning, with a little help from his now friend Eugene, to the plan.

Scene 48: Concert Hall

Vincent and Irene at the concert

Jerome and Irene are watching a concert pianist play the grand piano. It is a Chopin Sonata. Their hands touch and she looks shyly at him. As the music continues on the soundtrack, we cut to:

Scene 49: Gattaca, exterior, night

The investigator and Hugo are walking along a wire fence. Behind the fence, in a compound, we see police checking the identity of 'in-valids'. The investigator tells Hugo that he is looking in the wrong place. He tells Hugo that they should draw a five-mile radius around Gattaca and check everyone's identity.

Scene 50: Outside Jerome's apartment, night

Another near 'miss'

A policeman is checking Eugene's identity. Up on the screen comes the identity of Jerome Morrow. The detective notices that he is listed as a navigator and asks about the wheelchair. Swiftly, Eugene turns the tables, claiming that he has hurt his leg, and questioning the policeman's right to check him. As the detective goes off mumbling apologies, Eugene abuses him for his impertinence.

Scene 51: Gattaca centre, night

Detectives see Caesar collecting trash. They take the bag from him.

Scene 52: Concert hall, night

The pianist – an 'imperfect' specimen

The pianist finishes the piece. He stands and acknowledges the audience's applause. Then he throws his white gloves to the audience. Jerome (Vincent) catches one. Irene puts it on. There is an extra finger.

Outside the hall, they both look at a poster of the pianist, who has twelve fingers. She remarks that the piece needs twelve fingers to be played properly.

Scene 53: A road tunnel, night

Another near 'miss'

Police are checking all the cars that are coming through the tunnel. Irene and Jerome (Vincent) are in one of the cars. Looking ahead, Jerome sees that the police are checking for any unusual signs, including looking at people's eyes. He removes his contact lenses, and drops them on the ground. The police approach the car. They ask for a mouth swab. Jerome avoids that, saying he would give them a contaminated sample (he lies that he is drunk). They take a blood sample from his finger instead. It tests valid and shows his Jerome Morrow identity. They are allowed through the police blockade.

Scene 54: Street, night

Vincent nearly killed

Irene stops the car. She tells Jerome (Vincent) she wants to show him something. She gets out of the car and crosses the road. Jerome, without his contact lenses, cannot see a thing. She calls him to come across the busy road. He cannot move for fear of being run over by a car he cannot see. Finally, he clumsily rushes across the road, narrowly missing being hit. He joins her at the other side.

Scene 55: Mirror farm

She leads him up a ladder and shows him the sight. It is a field of mirrors. Slowly the sun comes up. They look on in awe.

Later, the sun completely up, they walk along a row between the mirrors. She tells him his eyes look different, and he lies that it is just the light.

Commentary The thriller-style tension is maintained, with several more dramatic 'near misses' (Eugene's identity, the police roadblock, the lost contact lenses). In terms of what the film is arguing, three scenes stand out as highly significant.

First there is the concert. The revelation about the pianist having six fingers makes an obvious point about the usefulness of genetic imperfection. This individual, who would be classed as abnormal, or invalid, produces beautiful music. The music itself acts as a type of argument for 'imperfection', when we think about it.

Second, there is the road crossing scene. Jerome (Vincent)

cannot see to protect himself. To cross the road blindly is to invite the possibility of death. Every instinct in him cries out against it. Yet he cannot (at this stage) betray his identity to Irene. He must take the risk, if the false identity is to be protected. And thus he risks all. It is a kind of variation on the swimming race scene: his determination has now been put to another (and the ultimate) test, and once more he triumphs.

Finally, there is the mirror farm scene. This is a strange one, and perhaps strains credibility. But it is clearly symbolic. Clearly, it points to the stars, in both a literal and metaphoric sense: literal because our sun is one of the stars; metaphoric, because the sun is often taken as symbolic of gold, life, aspirations, and other qualities that transcend the mundane life we normally live. This scene connects with Vincent's 'dream' (looking to space, as in Scenes 5, 13 and others) and the several scenes in which the stars feature. It reminds us that a wish to achieve, to get 'above' our predestined fate, is part of what makes us fully human, and finally more important than any genetic code.

Scene 56: Investigator's home, night

The Chief Investigator is exercising in his mini pool when the phone rings. He answers it. It is Detective Hugo.

Scene 57: Police lab, night

The net closes Hugo explains that they have now found another sample of the invalid (Vincent). It is too much of a coincidence that two such samples can be found within two days. Hugo recommends an intravenous test of all employees. The investigator protests, but Hugo insists that it is the only way to be sure.

Scene 58: Gattaca medical centre

Vincent just escapes detection All employees are waiting in line for the intravenous blood test. Detective Hugo assures his boss that it's only a matter of time. Inside the medical centre, the doctor takes a blood sample from Jerome's arm. Jerome (Vincent) has a vial of blood hidden in his hand. He pretends that the doctor has hurt him, jumps up and swiftly exchanges the blood vial. The doctor tests the sample, and it shows Jerome's valid identity.

Scene 59: Gattaca, outside the medical centre

Jerome emerges. Irene ironically congratulates him on not being the murderer. He tells her that he is leaving in two days and looks at her questioningly. She smiles at him. Meanwhile Hugo, the chief investigator and the director are standing together as the last of the employees leaves. They have found nothing. Hugo is convinced that they have missed something and recommends that they test again. At this point the director intervenes, saying that they only have a seven day window of opportunity in seventy years, and he cannot allow any more disruption. Hugo notes that the previous director (the dead man) opposed the launch program, implying that the director might have had a motive. The director replies that his gene profile will show that he has not a violent bone in his body. The investigator apologises, and tells Hugo that they will have to look elsewhere.

Scene 60: Jerome's apartment, night

Jerome has been collecting samples. He blows up a medical glove and lets it go, bored.

Scene 61: Nightclub

Vincent and Irene in love

Irene and Jerome are sitting together at the table. She takes a heart tablet. She comments on the fact that he must know little of such imperfections. He tells her she would be surprised. She jokes that perhaps he might only ever had have his heart broken. They dance. He tells her that it is funny that he has tried so hard to get out of a place (Gattaca), only at the last moment to find a reason to stay. They look at one another, and are on the point of kissing.

At that moment, the detectives appear. Hugo announces that everyone is to stay and be checked. They make a run for it. The investigator picks up Irene's heart tablet pill box.

Scene 62: Back alley outside nightclub, night

Vincent on the run

Irene and Jerome (Vincent) come out of the nightclub. At the foot of the stairs is a detective. Jerome suddenly punches the man, and follows up with several blows and a kick. Dragging Irene he runs down the alleyway. Hugo and the others come out and find the man. Hugo immediately orders mouth and other samples (to find out who the assailant was). Down the alleyway Jerome has dragged Irene into a recessed area. The investigator suddenly calls out, 'Vincent!'

In hiding, Irene asks who Vincent is. Before Jerome can reply, she tells him to say nothing. They kiss, passionately.

Scene 63: Irene's house, night

With the waves crashing on the beach in the background, we see Irene and Jerome (Vincent) making love.

Next morning, Jerome awakes, beside Irene. He spots a hair on the pillow. He begins to look for other traces.

Scene 64: Beach, day

Jerome, naked, is pumicing himself with a stone and trying to wash off all traces of surface evidence. He is in despair.

Scene 65: Irene's house, day

Irene has woken up. Jerome is getting dressed. She notices the scars on his legs. He explains them away as an accident with a car. She tells him she believes he had something to do with the director's death. He replies that that is not true.

Commentary Two plot lines are intersecting in these scenes: the romantic story (Jerome/Vincent and Irene) and the investigation. Both create drama, and stress. The fact that Vincent's true identity has been discovered (Scene 62) is the moment he (and we, sympathising with him) have dreaded. On the other hand, his relationship with Irene has now reached its long anticipated climax. Yet she knows he has a secret, and suspects that it might involve the murder. Thus the two storylines draw us on – to what we expect to be the film's resolution.

Scene 66: Police centre

The chief investigator is looking at the screen images of Vincent and Jerome, interchanging them rapidly. Hugo comes in. He asks if this was the man from last night, only to get the reply that 'it's nobody'.

Scene 67: Gattaca navigation centre, day

The investigation targets 'Jerome' A detective is prising a key off the keyboard, looking for evidence. The director protests that Jerome Morrow is one of their best people. At that moment Irene walks into the room, and overhears Jerome's name. She goes out again. She intercepts Jerome coming towards the room.

She tells him that he is feeling sick and should go home. The investigator catches up with her and asks about Jerome. She explains that Jerome is sick. He persists, saying that he should visit Jerome and asking directions.

Scene 68: Police medical centre

Detective Hugo is looking again at the corpse of the director. He takes a sample and analyses it.

Scene 69: Gattaca centre

The investigator is standing beside the car with Irene. He puts her pill box on top of the car so that she can see it. Ironically he says, 'You don't know who he is, do you Irene?'

Scene 70: Gattaca centre, a corridor, day

Jerome phones Eugene about the investigator coming. We cut to Eugene at the apartment. Jerome tells Eugene that he (Jerome) is meant to be sick. He adds that there is very little time to prepare.

Scene 71: Jerome's apartment, day

Eugene forced to play 'Jerome' for Vincent

Eugene looks desperately up the staircase. He throws himself out of the wheelchair and begins to pull himself laboriously up the stairs. We cut to:

Scene 72: Road, day

The investigator is driving Irene along the road.

Scene 73: Jerome's apartment, day

We cut back to the apartment, where Eugene is pulling himself slowly and painfully up the staircase. (Scenes 72 and 73 are repeated).

Scene 74: Outside the apartment, day

The investigator and Irene arrive. They leave the car and walk to the apartment. The investigator rings the buzzer.

Scene 75: Jerome's apartment, day

Inside, Eugene is still struggling the last few paces. He reaches the intercom and invites them up. He crawls across to a chair, pulls himself up, rearranges himself and awaits them.

The investigator and Irene walk in. Eugene greets her as 'sweetheart', and asks for a kiss. Surprised, she nonetheless goes across and kisses him. Anton demands a blood sample. He takes the blood with a syringe and puts it into the hand-held testing instrument. The result is a picture of Jerome and the word "Valid". Still suspicious, Anton begins to look around the apartment. He walks down the stairs. We see that Jerome (Vincent) is hiding behind a pillar at the foot of the stairs. Just as Anton is sure to see him, he receives a call from Detective Hugo, with news that a man has been caught. Immediately, Anton leaves.

The near exposure of 'Jerome'

Jerome comes slowly up the stairs. Both men look at the stunned Irene. She leaves the apartment without a word.

Scene 76 – Outside the apartment, day

Vincent confesses the truth to Irene

Jerome catches up with Irene. He grabs her. She doesn't want anything to do with him. He admits that he is a 'god child', Vincent Freeman, but tells her he is the same person that he was yesterday – and not a murderer. He tells her that they have something in common, and places her hand on his chest. The difference is, he says, that he has less time than her – he is already 10,000 beats overdue (for death). He tells her, '**I am here to tell you that it *is* possible**'. Irene looks at him long and hard, and walks off.

Commentary The scenes leading to the near exposure of Eugene (and therefore Vincent) are full of the sort of excitement we expect in thrillers. That the pretence now comes to include Irene, who has her own suspicions of Jerome (Vincent), and instinctively lies (and breaks the law) to protect him adds another layer of tension. The suspense is relieved at the last moment by the phone call from Hugo, and news that the real culprit has been found. The 'whodunnit' elements of the film are strongly in play here, drawing us on.

Meanwhile, let us not ignore the character development. We see Eugene, for the first time ever, putting himself out in a major way to advance his friend's cause (the maintenance of the identity pretence). This is significant. Here was a man who was cynical, indifferent, wishing for death. Yet he has been caught up in the desperate plan, and finds himself committing, in that heroic struggle up the stairs, in a way we (and no doubt he) thought impossible. Eugene too has moved forward. Likewise, we see Irene tested, and come through with flying colours. She has put herself at risk for the sake of Jerome (Vincent). It is as if his daring, and drive, has now extended to effects on his friends.

And finally there is Vincent himself. At long last he admits the truth to Irene. She has guessed his identity of course. What she doesn't know is how 'imperfect' he is. That information he gives her in a genuine spirit of sharing with someone he loves. He has abandoned the pretence of perfection for the reality of being a 'battler'. But again the film makes a point. In doing so, Vincent doesn't diminish himself – he joins her – both literally (in their shared heart condition) and figuratively, in the company of people who accept what they really are.

Scene 77: Police centre

The real murderer identified

The Investigator goes into the centre, and into an interrogation room. Seated at a table is Director Josef. Detective Hugo informs his boss that spittle from the Director was found in the dead man's eye. He was trying to save the missions, knowing that he would not live to see another one. The investigator is shocked, but relieved. Hugo looks at him knowingly, and says that he will undoubtedly be celebrating that night. The investigator leaves.

Scene 78: Jerome's apartment, day

Jerome carries Eugene down the stairs and puts him back in his wheelchair. Eugene is cocky and relieved. Jerome however asks about the detective and tells Eugene that it is not over: Vincent will have to meet the detective.

Scene 79: Gattaca centre, day

Vincent is confronted by the investigator (Anton)

Jerome (Vincent) walks into the navigation centre. A solitary figure is at his computer console. As he approaches, The investigator calls out, 'Vincent?' He turns and remarks on how much Vincent has changed. He tells Vincent that they are brokers, and that both their parents had died thinking he (Anton) had outlived his brother. When Vincent asks what he is doing there, Anton (the investigator) replies that he has a right to be there (being a police officer investigating), whereas Vincent does not. They shout at one another. Vincent still wants to go on with the mission, though Anton tells him he is guilty of fraud and that 'it's over'. Vincent reminds him that he needed rescuing once before. Anton replies that he beat himself. He asks if

Vincent wants him to prove it (that he is still superior). He insists.

Scene 80: Beach, night

The new sea trial

Slowly the two men take off their clothes. They plunge into the breaking waves. They swim through the sea, on and on. After a while, Anton calls out to Vincent, asking '**How have you done any of this?**' Vincent replies that it is closer to go to the other side.

Vincent's 'philosophy'

Anton asks where the other shore is. Vincent replies instead, '**You want to know how I did it...I never saved anything for the swim back.**'

A new triumph

Anton, in despair, turns back. After a moment, Vincent follows him. Anton however has run out of strength. Helpless, he sinks beneath the water. Vincent, coming to where he believes his brother to be and seeing no one, dives below the water. We see him grab the sinking body of Anton. Vincent pulls him to the surface. He begins the long swim back to shore, holding on to his brother. As he goes, he looks up at the stars. He pulls his brother out of the waves onto the shore.

Commentary The resolution of the 'whodunnit' subplot is satisfying, and ties off that part of the narrative. It also removes the shadow of a doubt we might have had about Vincent (was he involved somehow, but we hadn't found out?). But having the blame put on someone else doesn't get him 'off the hook' so far as his false identity is concerned. He has been caught at last! Yet, by a happy coincidence, the investigator is revealed to be his long lost brother. The hitherto surprising lack of information about the chief investigator (Anton) is now revealed to be a clever narrative ploy, keeping this surprise till last. But having his brother catch him is not the end of his problems. A battle of wills over what will happen next (a continued cover up, or removal of Vincent from the centre, and therefore from his 'dream') ensues – Anton driven by his duty, and loyalty to the system which has elevated him – Vincent driven by his need to fulfil his long-held ambition. In a way which is obviously highly symbolic and thematically interesting, insofar as it revisits the 'valid' 'in-valid' distinction which first appeared in childhood, and the swimming dare which was their way then of proving themselves, the two men agree to one last swim.

At this point, we have no way of knowing what will happen. Vincent won the battle of wills in Scene 16, but can he endure that trial again (in the light particularly of Scene 44)? The resolution is in his favour, and once again Niccol signposts the underlying idea: 'I never kept anything in reserve for the swim back' (translated: I never put anything less than 100% into my efforts – that's how I won). The heroism of the rescue, and above all the pointed reference to the stars (ambition, aspiration, winning) make the idea quite explicit. It is another triumph for Vincent's indomitable spirit. By the way, it is also a rebonding of the brothers, a triumph of the relationship which brings the two men together, over the scientific classification which would keep them apart (blood over genes, one might say).

Scene 81: Street, night

Irene is fast asleep in her car. She wakes up. She looks in the rear vision mirror and sees Vincent. She tells him she understands that he could not see when he crossed the road that night – 'but you crossed it anyway'. He plucks out a hair and hands it to her, saying, '**If you're still interested, let me know**'. She pauses, then drops the hair and says, 'Sorry…' Vincent looks downcast. She adds, '**The wind blew it**'. He smiles.

Irene accepts Vincent as he is

Scene 82: Irene's apartment

Irene and Vincent are in bed together. She kisses him tenderly.

Commentary The murder mystery has been resolved. The relationship with Anton has been resolved. That leaves the matter of Irene. She effectively rejected Vincent (Scene 76), whether because she had heard he was imperfect, or because she felt aggrieved at being part of the deceit, we don't know. Now he re-presents himself to her, without any pretence – as the *real* Vincent. And she accepts him. The throwing away of the hair is a symbolic acceptance of him (regardless of his genetic inferiority), and his love. Again, we read the subtext: it is who you are, and what relationships you have, that matter – *not* your gene code.

Scene 83: Jerome's apartment, night

Vincent walks through the deserted apartment. All the apparatus for the faking of identity is covered. Jerome (Eugene) greets Vincent (Jerome). He leads him and shows him a fridge full of samples – 'enough for two lifetimes'. He tells Vincent 'I'm travelling too.' Vincent thanks Jerome, who replies, '**I got the better end of**

Eugene's testimony to Vincent

the deal. I only lent you my body. You lend me your dream.' Jerome hands Vincent an envelope, to be opened when he gets 'upstairs'.

Scene 84: Gattaca centre

The final obstacle

Vincent joins other staff. The doctor is waiting for him, insisting on another sample. Vincent is taken completely by surprise, unprepared. Reluctantly, he provides the urine sample, knowing the deceit is over. The doctor however is talking throughout about his son, who wants to come to Gattaca too. The only trouble is, **'He is not all that they promised – but then – who knows what he could do?'**. Still not understanding, Vincent gives the doctor the sample. The machine comes up with Vincent's (invalid) identity. The doctor looks at Vincent, and tells him that for future reference he should hold 'it' with his right hand if he is pretending to be a right handed man. The doctor changes the identity to that of Jerome. **'I was as good as any and better than most...I could have gone up and back and no one would have been the wiser.'** **'You'll miss your flight, Vincent,'** he says.' Finally understanding, Vincent goes off. He looks back in gratitude.

Success

Vincent makes his way through a long corridor which ends at the launch facility. He climbs through a sealed door, and joins the crew in the space capsule.

Commentary

What Vincent (Jerome) discovers when Doctor Lamar accepts his fake identity is (by implication) how widespread the disenchantment with the Gattaca system is. Here is another person (like the gene broker, Jerome, Irene, perhaps Caesar) who is willing to subvert the system because he sees how unjust it is. This complicity of deception, illegal though it may be, is clearly signposted by the filmmaker as positive, humane, entirely proper in the context. The references to the doctor's son, the joke, and above all Vincent's look of gratitude, tell us what amounts to this: in an unjust system, breaking the law is a legitimate act of protest and humanity.

Scene 85: Jerome's apartment, night

Jerome pulls himself into the cleansing chamber. He adjusts himself and puts his swimming medallion round his neck. Then he reaches out. We cut back to Vincent entering the rocket.

Scene 86: Gattaca launch centre, night

Vincent leaves Earth

We cut to the blast of flame as the rocket takes off. Inside the capsule, Vincent and the other crew are off into space. The rocket flies through the night sky.

Scene 87: Jerome's apartment, night

Jerome dies

We see the flames in the chamber consuming Jerome.

Scene 88: Space capsule

In the space capsule, Vincent is silently contemplating what he has achieved, with the help of Jerome. He opens the envelope. It contains a lock of Jerome's hair. The voice over says, '**For someone who was never meant for this world, I must confess I'm suddenly having a hard time leaving it. Of course they say every atom in our bodies was once part of a star. Maybe I'm not leaving. Maybe**

'Going home'

I'm going home.' We see the screen full of stars.

The credits roll.

Commentary How are we to read Jerome's suicide? As the despicable act of a 'loser'? Or as the deliberate choice of someone who has chosen his own destiny, just as Vincent chose his. The pairing of the death scenes (85 and 87) with those showing Vincent achieving his goal at last (86 and 88) points us towards the more noble interpretation. The fire of the incinerator, the fire of the rocket; Jerome with his precious medallion, Vincent with the lock of hair from his friend; Jerome asserting himself, Vincent asserting himself. The finale of the movie is unquestionably affirming, though with a bitter-sweet tinge.

And as Vincent goes off into the stars, he experiences contentment. He has proven himself, bucked the system (for good reason, the film suggests), transcended his genetic destiny, and in so doing becomes an exemplar in the closing moments of what the film is saying: you can achieve whatever you want, define your own fate, if only you have the willpower and the imagination (to dream). The triumphant tone – of the words, the vision, and the music – draw our attention to the film's message and give it a sort of resonance that can stay in our memories.

Notes on Characters

Vincent Freeman (Jerome Morrow) – Ethan Hawke

The two sides of Vincent
Two opposing elements define Vincent. One is his poor genetic profile – his congenital heart problem, his myopia, his physical stature. This is established with brutal clarity only moments after his birth, in the damning printout read by the nurse. 'Life expectancy – 30 years'. The other however is his extraordinary psychological strength – his ambition and urge to succeed. This is established first by means of the scene (11) in which he angrily rubs out the superior height mark for brother Anton, then by his mapping out of the 'dream' of being an astronaut.

Everything else in his story proceeds from these two fundamentals. All his problems flow from his poor genes – the (initially) low self-esteem, the career exclusion, the need for deception, the constant risk of being exposed as the impostor inside Gattaca. But all his actions, once he rebels against the *Vincent's struggle to succeed* 'hand' destiny has dealt him (Scene 16), are driven by his commitment to the dream. Niccol is canny enough to show the struggle involved – Vincent does not achieve his success easily. The first swimming scene (12) shows him losing to Anton, because (it is implied) he accepts the notion of his inferiority. It is only later that he decides to fight back – and ends up winning the race (16). Twice, once he has embarked on his 'Jerome' deception, he nearly gives up completely – when the gene broker confronts him with the surgical saw (25), and when he realises that he is the prime murder suspect in the investigation (46). In both cases, it is Eugene who brings him back to his plan, and his commitment.

The love story
Vincent's story is not just about his struggle to succeed. There is also the love story – the developing relationship with Irene. But in a sense this is a variation on the same theme. In succeeding with her he is likewise triumphing over his genetic fate – for she is genetically 'superior' to him, and that is finally out in the open for both of them. The Vincent-Irene romance is also another way for Niccol to explore the conflicting ideas of discrimination and tolerance. Vincent accepts her supposed inferiority (45), and later she accepts his (81). In both cases, the filmmaker argues that

people should be judged by emotional, moral and relationship yardsticks, not just by genetic profiling (physical in this case). Thus the romance ties back into the main proposition of the script – that qualities of mind measures and character are what's important – not just biology.

Jerome Morrow (Eugene) – Jude Law

If Vincent acts as an exemplar of the human spirit in the ascendant, then Jerome (Eugene) is on the opposite side of the ledger. He lacks the will to succeed, and it costs him dearly.

Jerome as a representation of failure of will

Jerome was genetically superior, and could 'do anything'. Yet he didn't have the mental focus. Coming second in the swimming championships, despite his biological superiority, points to a lapse in commitment, a lack of 'will'. This leads to the attempted suicide, the disablement, the half life, the deception (handing his body over to Vincent) and finally to the second (and successful) suicide. Niccol is making a very pointed comparison between Eugene and Vincent: one had everything physically, but lacked motivation; the other was chronically disadvantaged, but had remarkable motivation.

Yet Jerome/Eugene is not there just as a negative contrast with the hero, as an example of the failure of spirit. He actually *changes* in the course of the narrative. Our first glimpse of Jerome (24) shows him to be a person hunched bitterly in his wheelchair, smoking and staring icily into the distance. He has accepted the 'deal' brokered by German out of desperation, and is doing it only for the money.

The significance of the change in Jerome

This chilly disdain continues for some time. However, as the deceit goes on, and Jerome witnesses Vincent's struggle – including the two moments of crisis when he nearly gives up completely – we sense him being drawn into the whole 'dream' (Eugene's word). He finds himself inspired. He also becomes, against the grain of his old arrogance, a genuine friend of Vincent. The restaurant scene, when Vincent (Jerome) asks him what he will do in the year he is in space, suddenly alerts us to the real bond that has developed between the two men. (The non-reply is also, of course, an early pointer to the plan to commit suicide.) The biggest test of Eugene's friendship perhaps is the 'substitution' scene (75), in which he has to crawl up the stairs and impersonate the physically whole Jerome (Vincent). Now this could be put down to just continuing the deceit, but there is something subliminally heroic about the way he does it. The very act of dragging himself up is itself symbolic. He is actually trying to achieve something – putting himself out – for the first time in years. All this comes to a head in two scenes: when he tells Vincent 'I'm proud of you' (39), and when he thanks Vincent and gives him the locket of hair (83). Jerome (Eugene) has been influenced, if only for a time, by the gutsy example of his friend, and it has made him a better person.

The suicide

Why then does he commit suicide? Is it because he can't live without Vincent? Is it a lapsing back into his old despair? Or is it a sort of 'euthanasia', in which he chooses death rather than the dishonour of continuing to be a useless cripple? The film does not give us explicit guidelines on this point, but it does signal that the death of Jerome (Eugene) is a triumph. The fire which blasts Vincent off to the stars is given an obvious visual parallel in the fire which consumes Eugene. Vincent has his space mission (his present triumph); Eugene has his medallion (symbolic of his past triumph). The locket of hair links the two men in this climactic moment, affirming something very positive. Somehow it seems fitting, at a quasi-mythical level, that Eugene asserts himself in one last act (though it be death). And his words ring in our ears: 'I only lent you my body. You lent me your dream.'

Irene – Uma Thurman

Irene functions primarily as the love interest in *Gattaca*, the beautiful woman whom Vincent pursues and attains. She adds glamour and emotional fuel to the narrative. The coming together of the two is admirably shown in the two love scenes (63 and 82), offering viewers a very traditional pleasure – that of vicariously sharing a romance.

Irene also has another function. Beneath the appearance of (physical) perfection, she is a variation on the idea of human 'imperfection'. In her case, it is a heart disorder that prevents her from going into space (as she desires). This is her embarrassed secret, the source of her dismay when she realises that Jerome (Vincent) is apparently a superman (37). What the filmmaker is positioning us to feel is of course significant. We think – well she *may* be 'imperfect', but who cares? And Vincent thinks exactly the same. That's the point of his throwing away the hair (rejecting her genetic inferiority). Herein lies the text's message. Genetic perfection is not the point. It's what a *person* is like – whether you can relate to them or not – their intrinsic worth as a human being.

This message reverberates throughout the film – in the whole

Irene as an imperfect specimen

deceit of Vincent, in the collusion of others with him in that deceit, in Irene's eventual (knowing) acceptance of him as imperfect too – and we begin to sense that the idea is very broad. What Niccol is saying is that judging people according to some external standard leads to inhumanity. The film makes subliminal references to totalitarian or police states, and we remember that it was racial (a cruder form of genetic) discrimination that led to the gas chambers.

The imperfection theme

The Irene-Vincent relationship revolves thematically round two assertions of this principle: he refuses to judge Irene as deficient, because he loves her (45); she (later) refuses to judge Vincent as deficient, because she loves him (81). In so doing, they choose humanity and individuality over what the film suggests are erroneous, belittling, cruel standards. And their love emotionally underpins the strength of this message.

Anton Freeman (The investigator) – Loren Dean

Anton is to some extent a plot device. The fact that his true identity is not revealed till the end keeps up the narrative suspense. That he is the long lost brother is a convenient development, insofar as it relocates the drama to the old childhood rivalry, and allows Vincent to win through after all.

When we think back, Anton has several times tried to put Hugo 'off the scent', and retrospectively we realise that he was trying to protect Vincent. Why? Because they are brothers, and 'blood is thicker than water'. It argues a *personal* reason for siding with Vincent, not just the official reason, and once more (in parallel with Eugene, Irene, possibly Caesar and certainly Dr Lamar), we see a principle other than genetic perfection being applied in human affairs. It goes without saying that we are invited to congratulate Anton on his collusion, because the film has long since made out a powerful case that Vincent is right (in trying to fulfil his own potential) and the system is wrong (in trying to deny him his rights).

Anton – another rebel against the system

Anton also serves as a kind of 'proof' that the genetic profiling regime is not an exact predictor anyway: if it was, Vincent could not have won the race. Anton's defeat in the sea encodes another criticism of the false truth of science as the measure of all things.

Notes on Themes and Issues

The dangers of genetic engineering and scientific experimentation

Quote

I would hate for anyone to look at my film and think it is advocating that you never tamper with genes, because there have been and will be many positive things to come out of this kind of science in terms of curing diseases. But the problem is that blurred line between health and enhancement. How far do you go? Do you consider short-sightedness a disease? Premature balding? Crooked teeth? Where do you draw the line? (Andrew Niccol, Screenwriter and Director of *Gattaca*)

Discovery of DNA

Subsequent technological developments

'Gattaca' – a DNA society

In 1953, Nobel prize winners James Watson and Francis Crick discovered what Crick called 'the secret of life'. It was the basic model of all genetics, the double helix DNA structure at the heart of all cells. Watson and Crick were awarded the Nobel Prize for this monumental discovery (1962), for they had unlocked one of the great secrets of science. On it has been built all the bio-technical developments which have since defined our world: the identification of which genes define the characteristics of all organisms (1969 onwards), the synthesis of genes (1970), the beginning of true genetic engineering (1976), genetic 'fingerprinting' (1984), the genetic modification of animals (1988), the development of genetically modified food (1994), the cloning of a live animal ('Dolly' the sheep in 1997), stem cell research (1998) and other forms of gene therapy. And all these developments raise ethical questions, which have been quite controversial. The discovery of DNA had set the scene for what has become a major scientific and social issue in our society.

Gattaca takes its name from the DNA blueprint for all life. In every cell of every living thing, a spiral of *deoxyribose nucleic acid* (DNA for short) is encoded with all the genetic information for that living thing. The spiral is made up of interlocking chemicals – an outer rim made up of phosphate and sugar 'nucleotides' – an inner structure comprising four different nitrogen elements – **guanine**, **adenine**, **thymine** and **cystosine**. Scientists give these chemicals letter symbols to simplify the writing down of the code: P and S (for the phosphate and sugar rim) and **G**, **T**, **C** and **A** for the nitrogen 'blocks'. It is the nitrogen elements which vary, and therefore define genetic makeup. Since the P and S blocks are a constant, only the nitrogens are written down, using the letters G, A, T and C. A sequence might be: GGAATTAACCAA. Hence the name of the society which is based on genetic perfection: Gattaca. In the title sequence, the A's, C's G's and T's are bolded – a subtle clue to his idea.

The proposition of the script

The proposition of genetic selection mounted by the film is a slightly far-fetched one, mainly because identification of all the 'imperfect' genes, in all the fertilised ova, in all the 'test tube babies', would be an exhaustive, expensive and probably imprecise process. The idea of genetic engineering – that is of 'cutting and pasting' the best DNA from the parents to make perfect babies – is even more problematical. One American geneticist, on seeing *Gattaca*, commented 'There's not a chance in hell that you could recombine all those genes and get a desired effect'. But SF is not so much about current state technology as about what might be. It often works too by exaggerating a trend to the point where it is obviously intolerable, as with the film's depiction of a society ruled by 'genoism', and thereby inviting debate about what are real contemporary issues and potential problems.

Gattaca is really pointing us towards what is both a new and strangely enough an old controversy. The Human Genone Project, and all such research into finding the genetic profiles of common diseases (Parkinson's, Alzheimer's, etc) – and famous examples of genetic tinkering, such as the creation of 'Dolly' the sheep (a breakthrough 'clone' by Scottish geneticist Ian Willmut in 1997), alert us to how fast technology can take us into unchartered territory. But the issues involved are not that new.

Selective breeding

'Selective breeding' has long been established in agriculture and horticulture – the production of cows with higher milk yields and bigger roses for example – sees natural breeding being manipulated for genetically 'enhanced' effects. The use of genetically modified (GM) species – richer wheat, larger tomatoes, soy beans resistant to herbicides – is the same process, but with the intervention taking place at a molecular level. The latter has proved very controversial. It appears to open the 'Pandora's Box' of scientific experimentation, and raises that ancient and still haunting question: where will it lead? For instance, Greenpeace has publicly objected about 'the unknown DNA' in one of Nestlé's products, and expressed concern that 'its possible functions and effects…might pose a risk to human health and the environment'.

Human 'breeding'

If we turn to human selectiveness we move into even more troubling areas. Hitler famously asserted that the 'Aryan race' (by which he meant blue eyed, blond haired 'Nordic' types) were superior to all other racial variates. Nazi propaganda referred to such people as *Ubermensch* (superior men). The corollary, in the Nazi scheme of things, were those dubbed *Untermensch* (lesser beings, or under men), who quite simply needed to be got rid of, in order to achieve a racially 'pure', naturally superior Germany. The Nazis encouraged Aryan breeding programs, as well as of course exterminating the despised 'Semites' (Jews). This sort of thinking led directly to the death camps of the Holocaust, and the 6,000,000 murders committed under the Nazi's 'final solution' – the most notorious crime of the twentieth century. Human 'breeding' solutions do not have a good name. Images in the film resonate with these allusions or references.

Literary antecedents for the theme of breeding people

Literature and popular culture is full of dire warnings about scientific (and specifically biological) tinkering. Mary Shelley's 1816 masterpiece *Frankenstein* is all about an arrogant medical student (Victor Frankenstein) who builds a creature out of human body parts. The monster only wants to be normal, but is condemned to a terrible half life on the edge of society, and indeed is rejected by its maker – before it takes a terrible revenge. In 1896, H.G.Wells (author of *The Time Machine* and other great SF classics), wrote a novel called *The Island of Dr Moreau*. It concerns a mad scientist (Dr Moreau), who attempts to transform animals into humans. The misshapen results of his experiments eventually kill him. *Brave New World* (1932), Huxley's famous portrait of a future world of bottled babies and biological as well as psychological totalitarianism, is another landmark work.

Contemporary variations on the theme

All three works have inspired many movies and exerted a considerable influence on subsequent writing (*Blade Runner* and *Jurassic Park* are both for instance futuristic variations on *Frankenstein* and *Gattaca* itself is clearly indebted to *Brave New World*). Innumerable modern SF novels (Cook's *Chromosome 6*,

Sawyer's *Frameshift*, Kress's *Beggars in Spain*, etc) are about experiments gone wrong, as as quite a few horror movies (*Godzilla*, *The Fly*, *Hollow Man*, etc). It seems that people worry about 'interfering with nature' (as Vincent's parents signficantly do in Scene 10 of the film).

The relevance of the theme

Gattaca's depiction of a future world is not as melodramatic as *Frankenstein* or as dire as *Blade Runner*. However, it shows what would happen if we took things too far. Niccol is certainly tapping into the wider concerns about how science is used (and abused). As one book warned:

Quote

Disturbing signs already exist that the biowizardry of gene therapy is vulnerable to expropriation and misuse, perhaps on a catastrophic scale, by corporate, political and institutional interests, whose interests may not coincide with those of society at large. (Lyon and Gorner, *Altered Fates: Gene Therapy and the Retooling of Human Life*)

The film is clearly expressing concern about what will happen if scientific 'tools' are used without social or ethical constraints. As the film's producers say: 'humans are discovering a God-like power to alter the world but may not have the moral understanding or prescience to see where such tinkering might take us'.

The injustice of discrimination and prejudice of social 'class'

Quote

We now have discrimination down to a science.

Antecedents for the theme in literature and film

It is not unusual for writers to attack social difference or stratification. Dickens did it repeatedly in his portraits of the lives of the wretched poor (*Oliver Twist* is a celebrated example), or of the dangers of desperate social climbing (*Great Expectations*). Serious movies deal with it from time to time. John Ford's adaptation of the Steinbeck novel *The Grapes of Wrath* (1939) is considered a classic, and it exposes the misery of the poor 'Okies' during the Great Depression.

Science fiction's treatment of discrimination

Science fiction novels and movies with a powerful social message are a rare breed, but they do exist. Huxley's celebrated 1932 novel *Brave New World* proposes a future of test tube babies manufactured quite deliberately in 'class' hierarchies – the Alphas, Betas, Gammas, Deltas and Epsilons (the Alphas being the super-smart and successful, the Epsilons being the semi-moronic underclass). The shocking thing about Huxley's vision is that he imagines a society so mechanistic that it has baby factories, and enrichment (as with the Alphas) and retardation (as with the Epsilons) as a deliberate socio-genetic policy. Ridley Scott's 1982 classic *Blade Runner* takes a sidelong glance at the issue in that it has an underclass left behind on Earth, eking out an existence in the garbage-strewn urban canyons and post-apocalyptic environmental wasteland, while all the well-to-do have escaped 'Off world'. Both *Blade Runner* and *AI* (1999) propose a human overclass and a synthetic human or 'replicant' underclass.

The relevance of 'Gattaca' to our world

With *Gattaca*, we face a more subtle variation on the idea of class. Out of a misguided sense of idealism, people have started using genetic engineering to produce 'perfect specimens'. These 'vitros' or 'made men' have come to dominate and rule the society. While discrimination is officially outlawed, in practice, human nature being what it is, the 'perfect' class have taken over completely, and the imperfect class have become human garbage.

Now Niccol is not really asking us to believe that this will happen. His actual intention is closer to home: prompting us to think about an issue which is very much alive *in our own world*. We have social stratification – it's just that it is 'natural' (or long established by the forces of history), rather than a scientifically-based novelty.

Australia as an example

Even in a supposedly 'classless' society like Australia, there are those whose inherited wealth, high levels of education, rich social networks and enhanced self-concept allow them to live a better than average existence. They might be dubbed 'the A demographic', the 'rich', the 'privileged' or a number of other things, but there is little doubt that these 'Alpha's' live a comfortable life. At the other end of the social scale are those whose inherited expectations of poverty and social marginalisation, whose low levels of education and poor self-concept condemn them to a life of frustration, plus (quite possibly) substance abuse and violence. They might be dubbed the 'poor', the 'underprivileged', the 'socially handicapped', but these 'Epsilons' suffer limitations every bit as galling as (and much more real than) Niccol's fictional 'in-valids'. Let's vary the quote slightly. Of any such person (in *our* world), it might be said, 'The only way you'll see the inside of a university is if you're cleaning it'.

Niccol's case against discrimination

By positioning us to empathise with Vincent, Niccol makes out a case against the social pressures which would exclude him. In extrapolating this theme from within the film to a broader context, we find ourselves thinking about all those pressures *in our own community* which 'keep people down'. It is not going to be genetic profiles *per se* – though the surface representation of genes may be important (tallness, beauty, belonging to the dominant racial group, etc). It is going to be things like speaking the 'wrong' way, wearing the 'wrong' clothes, having been to the 'wrong' school, having the 'wrong' self-concept, being the 'wrong' sex, or age, or ethnic background. At this level of debate, the film has much to say about exclusion, injustice and need for constant ethical vigilance.

Determinism or free will – to what extent is a person's destiny a matter of choice?

Quote

I was now a member of a particularly detested segment of society. One of those who refuses to play the hand that he was dealt. I am most commonly known as a 'borrowed ladder' or a 'de-gene-erate'.

Gattaca's argument

The central 'argument' of Gattaca, when we think about it, is that a person can overcome his (or her) genetic destiny. Vincent is born with quite serious physical defects, expected to have only a lowly job and predicted to die young. Instead, he challenges his defects and the predictions, entering the prestigeous Gattaca facility by a cunning deception (pretending to be a perfect specimen called Jerome Morrow), completing the course, and finally attaining the stars (both literally and metaphorically).

His battle with adversity is the major psychological narrative of *Gattaca*. We are invited as viewers to cheer his efforts, to groan at the obstacles put in his way, and to feel a kind of elation at his final triumph. In so doing, we subliminally accept the Vincent argument: that willpower, determination and courage *can* produce miracles – that individuals *can* determine their own destiny.

The ancient debate

But is Niccol offering us an inspiring case study in human potential, or trying to sell us a sweet myth? In grappling with this question, we find ourselves in the middle of the oldest debate in philosophy. For centuries, people have wondered: do we run our own lives according to our wishes, or are we manipulated by forces greater than ourselves (over which we have little or no control)?

Determinism

In ancient times, the gods were seen as ruling people's lives, for better or worse. Christianity (and the other great religions) substituted for this concept the idea of God as the controller of human destiny, though an interesting variation was that we have the 'free will' (choice) to be good or bad, and therefore to do well (under God's control) or come to nothing. Since modern science, the sources of 'determinism' have been relocated again, this time in our genes (our physical and psychological inheritance), in social class, in gender, in culture. The argument runs: We are the creatures of our environment (parents, society, culture, etc) – we become what they allow us to become, within patterns of expectation or motivation already laid down. Our choices are limited. We think we are free, but really we are bound.

Free will

On the other hand, many would argue that we *do* have the power to control our destiny.' There are many inspiring tales of people from massively 'disadvantaged' backgrounds who go on to 'make something of themselves', against all expectation, and triumph over adversity. Self-help gurus and a great many psychologists emphasise that *the way we think* about things has a great deal to do with *what we achieve*. If we set goals, confront our fears, develop a strategy, follow through, persist (despite knockbacks or challenges or mockery), we will almost certainly succeed. This is the *Gattaca* argument. Let's remember two vital quotes from the film:

Quote

There is no gene for fate [ie destiny is more than just genes. (Publicity for *Gattaca*)
[Jerome had everything he needed to succeed] except the desire to do so.

Niccol makes the point about 'self-determination' very clear in the opposition between Vincent and

Eugene. Towards the end, Eugene says:

> I got the better end of the deal. I only lent you my body – you lent me your dream. (Eugene)

What the film seems to argue – free will and choice

This makes explicit what has been obvious in a number of scenes – that having a 'dream' (or clear concept of what you want) is a massive advantage, sufficient to be life-changing. Vincent had the 'spirit' to challenge his destiny, and he won. Eugene was passive, and so, from being superior, he ended up losing everything. All, the film suggests, depends on willpower, determination. *Gattaca* makes out a classic argument for individualism.

Whether you accept this proposition is a personal matter. In this regard, *Gattaca* is either a reminder of a great truth – or a feel-good fairy story. It's up to you to decide.

Authoritarianism and Individualism – the eternal battle of all societies

> No one exceeds his potential. (The Director)

Gattaca depicts a world of scientific/genetic control so complete that it actually involves the 'creation' of people. What is unusual is that this is not superimposed by some higher authority, but emerges from the desires of the people themselves. In seeking genetic 'perfection', the Gattaca society has made that perfection the measure of all people, and perfect beings (the A class 'made men' or 'valids') the controllers of everything. It is nonetheless a kind of authoritarianism (strongly controlled social structure), even totalitarianism (total control). What does the film say about such control?

Critique of totalitarianism

It offers a strong critique of super-controlled societies. The residents of Gattaca are not represented as vital and happy in their 'perfection', and those on the outside ('in-valids') are plainly even worse off. One can't help but associate the world of Gattaca with totalitarian regimes. This impression is established with the early images of the workers going to work at the space centre – all looking the same, all ordered, all fairly emotionless. There is a sense of sterility. This totalitarian connotation is made more (historically) specific with the later images of the 'in-valid' workers, the fences and compounds. Nazi iconography is at work here. The intrusiveness of the constant blood sampling and heart monitoring, the omnipresent genetic scans (with images of individuals taken from some supercomputer database), the size of the buildings (dwarfing the people), the paranoid atmosphere associated with the investigation – all argue dissent from such a world, such a rigid, crushing social order. Though the movie is less oppressive than full-on authoritarian 'nightmare' scenarios (*Nineteen Eighty-Four*, for instance with its telescreens in every room and its portraits of 'Big Brother', or even *Blade Runner*, with its flying police cars, screening machines and air of madness) – it still instills in us a sense of repugnance with the way things have ended up.

Endorsement of individualism

In contrast, the film advocates the idea of individualism, indeed of 'bucking the system' when it is unjust or excessive. Vincent's triumphant subversion of the system is the key to this. He asserts his own needs, and breaks the social mould, in what is represented as a major triumph of the human will over conformity. Those aspects of the story that deny individuality are implicitly critiqued. Think of Vincent's father's shattering remark (Scene 14): 'Look, the only way you'll see the inside of a spaceship is if you're cleaning it'. Those aspects that enhance individuality are applauded. Think of how we are positioned to feel about Dr Lamar's rebellion (Scene 84) against the code in favour of both Vincent and his own son. For the first time in the film this character becomes a 'real person' – with feelings, needs, empathy – and we are invited to celebrate his 'conversion'.

Gattaca does not engage in the larger debate about how far individual liberties can go without destabilising society. Individualism, if it involves the sort of excess chronicled in films like *Mad Max* (with its rampaging outback neanderthals) or *A Clockwork Orange* (with its psychopath urban thugs), becomes its own problem – just as authoritarianism is a burden. But Niccol seems to imply that in our sophisticated technologically advanced world, there is greater risk of conformity and an overly rigid order, than of the reverse. For him, the individual is the hero, the system the oppressor. The right of each person is finally, in his view, more important than the need for law and order. It is another thought-provoking proposition, and the proper subject for much debate.

What the Critics Say

This is a character-driven suspense movie, a rarity in its own right, and it's a character-driven science fiction movie, which is rarer still. Hawke and the rest of the cast…are all strong. But it's the smart, profoundly insightful script that's *Gattaca's* star attraction….In a veritable desert of slipshod blockbusters, what a drink of water this is!

(At-A-Glance Film Reviews, www.rinkworks.com, 1997)

Science fiction is often sneered at by the pretentious amongst us. They claim it is mindless escapism and uses fantasy to disguise a lack of quality. *Gattaca* proves these sentiments to be false, once and for all. It is frighteningly believable in its technological and social predictions but still manages to tell an interesting story.

(www.ozcraft.com)

'There is no gene for the human spirit.' This is the tagline of the movie *Gattaca*, a film that searches deep within the heart of man. This is one of Ethan Hawke's strongest performances as a man who refuses to trust the odds, and relies on…sheer will to achieve his dreams….The performances only enhance, however, a wonderful script by first time writer/director Andrew Niccol. It deals with science fiction and the future in the best way, by exploring ideas. He quickly and easily presents a future not unimaginable, and truly existing in a 'not-too-distant-future'….Niccol addresses [the issues of genetic engineering], mostly dealing with the discrimination that would probably take place in society. The most subtle and yet important question he asks though is whether a man is truly the sum of his genes, or could his spirit somehow carry him beyond all expectations? Such thoughts are dealt with through intelligent characters given intelligent dialogue and placed within intelligent situations. It is interesting how such a thoughtful picture can be at the same time a real thriller to watch as well. *Gattaca* is one of my favourite movies because it is not afraid to address important issues that are truly current in modern society, and do it with great thought and heart.

(Internet Movie Database)

Andrew Niccol's earth-bound futurist science fiction film is a gentle polemic [argument] about the human spirit in a society where technology controls what nature once determined randomly....*Gattaca* carries a sense of George Orwell's vision of the world as it might have been half a century after he propounded *1984*. We now know it is not so, but Niccol's film very seriously puts the theory that humankind may now have the means to make it so. Which is a bit scary.

(Four stars rating, Dougal MacDonald, *Canberra Times*)

Imagine an Orwellian story presented with a cool, eerie precision...and you have some sense of *Gattaca*, a handsome and fully imagined work of cautionary futuristic fiction. Its subject is bigotry...The film's world revolves around strict conformity at places like the Gattaca Corporation....*Gattaca*, an impressively fine-tuned first feature from Andrew Niccol...succeeds as a scarily apt extension of present-day attitudes. But beyond the ingenuity of its premise, *Gattaca* also holds interest with its obsessive attention to detail... [such as] Gattaca's headquarters in Frank Lloyd Wright's Marin County Civic Centre. The building becomes a perfect reflection of the film's spare, controlled state of mind.

(Janet Maslin, *New York Times*)

It has been ages since we've had a sci-fi film that could match its style with substance on equal terms. Therefore *Gattaca* should be embraced by futuristic buffs as an absolute godsend, even if the gods are genetic engineers....That this icy yet inviting movie works at all is entirely due to the extraordinary risks taken by first-time director Andrew Niccol. He pumps *Gattaca* full of brains and removes virtually all brawn from the mix...A stunning production design awash with watery blues and sterile operating-theatre sets nails *Gattaca's* cold, convincing version of reality perfectly. This film is an outright downer, yet it has a strange, relaxing magic. Never has a bad time at the movies felt so good.

(*Herald Sun* review)

Sample Essay

'While Gattaca is a disturbing portrait of present and future social trends, it offers reassurance in celebrating the endurance of the human spirit.'

Discuss.

Apt introductory quote

'We had made discrimination into a science,' says Vincent's voice over early in *Gattaca*. This deft quote sums up two of the major issues Niccol critiques in his film: excessive social stratification (or oppression), and science gone slightly mad. Both are with us in our own time, and Niccol proposes in his challenging fiction

Close discussion of the topic

that they will only get worse. On the other hand, while the film is predominantly bleak in its predictions, it is by no means hopeless. Indeed, the protagonist's triumph over his circumstances is a key part of what the text is arguing. The 'human spirit', it suggests, remains strong, and can act as a counterbalance to the negative tendencies of an oppressive, controlling society.

*Sub-topic 1: disturbing aspects of **Gattaca***

The 'brave new world' of *Gattaca* is a chilling one. While on the surface it seems orderly and serene, in fact we rapidly understand that this is no ideal future, but a sort of Orwellian technostate which has effectively crushed individuality and feeling. 'Genoism' rules. So-called perfect specimens are the unchallenged Alpha class in society, while 'in-valids' – those whose genetic profiles lack something – languish in underpaid menial work. Vincent is the case study of discrimination – a boy born with imperfections who has been callously excluded from his preferred career because his genes don't read too well. 'The only way you'll see the inside of a spaceship is if you're cleaning it,' says his father bluntly, and it's the truth. The 'interview' he fails early on (before his secret deception) is the threat of a urine test. Meanwhile, the 'vitros' or 'made men' – those selected before birth for their perfect gene set – go on to their chosen futures without impediment. Gattaca shows them to be locked into a system which is like the very architecture – cold, empty, mechanical, conformist – a mockery of real life.

Sub-topic 2:
counter-
arguments

Yet the social order of *Gattaca* does not go unchallenged. In the example of Vincent, we see someone who recognises the injustice of the system, and is prepared to challenge it. The breakthrough comes when he realises that that 'I [knew] I was not as weak [as I believed]'. It is the first time Vincent saves his genetically superior brother Anton from drowning. It leads to a secret rebellion, and in due course to taking on Jerome Morrow's identity. If the system insists on blood and urine checks, Vincent will provide the perfect specimens demanded – Jerome's. In an illicit undercover operation, he masquerades as another person in order to beat the system and achieve his goal – going to the stars (itself a metaphor for personal achievement). Although Vincent's deception is against the law of this world, we, the viewers, cheer him on – following him through every crisis as he attempts to get 'up there'.

Sub-topic 3: How
the dilemma is
resolved

Until the last moment, practically, we are not sure who will win: the totalitarian order of Gattaca, or Vincent. The murder investigation accidentally exposes his identity, and he is in danger of being denounced. But by one of those remarkable plot devices, the investigator turns out to be his brother, and the matter is resolved by a renewed dare – another swim with highly symbolic overtones, in which Vincent demonstrates again his fierce determination and courage ('I never left anything in reserve for the swim back'), and incidentally saves Anton from drowning a second time.

Conclusion: both
aspects present
– the affirmative
is dominant

Thus, although *Gattaca* exposes and critiques a social order built on ruthless genetic selection – with its connotations of racism, class warfare and all kinds of unacceptable prejudice – it also allows its hero to triumph over this system. Vincent finally carries off his amazing subterfuge. He has challenged his genetic destiny, and the social path that should have been defined for him, proving himself superior to all the 'made men'. As he flies up towards the stars (both literally and figuratively), he finally senses that he is 'home', that is, fulfilled. He has braved much, and in so doing demonstrated how tenacious is the human will to succeed. The film ends with a glorious sense of wonder, and reaffirms the nobility of people's aspirations.

Sample Essay Questions

1. '*Gattaca* is a unusual mixture – an engrossing thriller with a strong social consience.'

   Do you agree with this assessment?

2. '*Gattaca* draws us into its paranoid world and makes this frightening future convincing.'

   How?

3. 'Vincent is supposed to be weak. Yet his strength of character is the key to the story.

   Discuss.

4. 'Without dreams we are nothing: that is what *Gattaca* argues.'

   Do you agree?

5. '*Gattaca* shows us the dangers of uncontrolled technology.'

   Discuss.

6. '*Gattaca* is about the triumph of the human spirit.'

   Is it?

Titles in this series so far

The Accidental Tourist
Angela's Ashes
Antigone
Away
The Bell Jar
Blade Runner
The Blooding
Breaker Morant
Briar Rose
Brilliant Lies
The Brush-Off
Cabaret
Cat's Eye
The Chant of Jimmie Blacksmith
Cloudstreet
The Collector
Cosi
The Crucible
The Divine Wind
Diving for Pearls
Educating Rita
Elli
Emma & Clueless
Falling
Fly Away Peter
Follow Your Heart
The Freedom of the City
Frontline
Gattaca
Girl with a Pearl Earring
Going Home
A Good Scent from a Strange Mountain
Great Expectations
The Great Gatsby
Hamlet
The Handmaid's Tale
Hard Times
Henry Lawson's Stories
Highways to a War
I for Isobel
An Imaginary Life
In Between
In Country
In the Lake of the Woods
The Inheritors
The Journey Area of Study
King Lear
The Kitchen God's Wife
A Lesson before Dying

Letters from the Inside
The Life and Crimes of Harry Lavender
Lives of Girls and Women
The Longest Memory
Looking for Alibrandi
The Lost Salt Gift of Blood
Macbeth
Maestro
A Man for All Seasons
Medea
Montana 1948
My Brother Jack
My Left Foot
My Name is Asher Lev
My Place
Night
Nineteen Eighty-Four
No Great Mischief
Oedipus Rex
Of Love and Shadows
One True Thing
Only the Heart
Othello
The Outsider
Paper Nautilus
The Player
Pride and Prejudice
Rabbit-Proof Fence
Raw
Remembering Babylon
The Riders
Schindler's List
Scission
Shakespeare in Love
The Shipping News
Sometimes Gladness
Stolen
Strictly Ballroom
Summer of the Seventeenth Doll
Things Fall Apart
Tirra Lirra by the River
Travels with my Aunt
We All Fall Down
What's Eating Gilbert Grape
The Wife of Martin Guerre
Wild Cat Falling
Witness
Women of the Sun
Wrack